T0386775

RMS
TITANIC
IN 50 OBJECTS

About the Contributors

Formed in the late 1990s, WHITE STAR MEMORIES has become one of the world's leading *Titanic* and White Star Line exhibition companies, with a privately owned collection comprising well over 1,000 artefacts, including the rare and unique. Specialising in the opulence and splendour of *Titanic* and her sister ships, its exhibitions have been appreciated by millions across the world. Indeed, as the *Titanic* phenomenon continues to grow, so does its incredible collection.

BRUCE BEVERIDGE is one of the foremost visual and technical historians of the *Olympic*-class ships. His highly sought-after General Arrangement plan of *Titanic*, released in 2003, is one of the most detailed and accurate plans released to date and has subsequently been used by dive teams investigating the wreck. He has advised on *Titanic's* specifications for news media, publishers, scale-model manufacturers, archivists, exhibitors and television production companies across the world. He frequently gives talks and presentations globally and also makes regular appearances in *Titanic* documentaries.

STEVE HALL is a historian, author, novelist and renowned *Titanic* researcher. He is one of the world's foremost authorities on her photographic record, having collected, studied and researched the ship for over three decades, and is a recognised authority on the technical aspects of the *Olympic*-class ships. He is a consultant for media centres, auction houses and museums around the world and is regularly invited to conduct talks with history students. He is a foundation member of the Titanic and Steamship Historical Society of Australia.

Together Beveridge and Hall have over sixty years of experience in researching *Titanic* and are her most prolific co-author team. They were founding trustees of the Titanic Research & Modeling Association, once the most-valued resource on her engineering, construction and operation. Their writing partnership has produced such books as *Titanic in Photographs* and the epic two-volume set *Titanic: The Ship Magnificent*, and they have also contributed to numerous documentaries, such as *Rebuilding Titanic*, *Titanic The Mission* and *Save The Titanic*.

RMS
TITANIC
IN 50 OBJECTS

BRUCE BEVERIDGE & STEVE HALL

The History Press

Dedicated to Stephen Larkin

Cover Illustration: One of the last surviving White Star lifeboats
(Brian Thompson).

First published 2022

The History Press
97 St George's Place, Cheltenham,
Gloucestershire, GL50 3QB
www.thehistorypress.co.uk

© Bruce Beveridge & Steve Hall, 2022

The right of Bruce Beveridge & Steve Hall to be identified as
the Authors of this work has been asserted in accordance with
the Copyright, Designs and Patents Act 1988.

All rights reserved. No part of this book may be reprinted
or reproduced or utilised in any form or by any electronic,
mechanical or other means, now known or hereafter invented,
including photocopying and recording, or in any information
storage or retrieval system, without the permission in writing
from the Publishers.

British Library Cataloguing in Publication Data.
A catalogue record for this book is available from the British Library.

ISBN 978 0 7509 9855 0

Typesetting and origination by The History Press
Printed and bound in Great Britain by TJ Books Limited, Padstow,
Cornwall.

Trees for Life

Contents

Foreword by Cathy Akers-Jordan   9
Author's Introduction   11

Part I: The Owners and Builders

1   White Star Line Advertising Brochure for *Olympic*
        and *Titanic*   17
2   Harland & Wolff Builder's Plate   24

Part II: *Titanic* Conceived

3   White Star Line Advertising Brochure   29
4   Rivets from the Construction Berths of *Titanic*
        and *Olympic*   33
5   No. 401: *Titanic*'s Rigging Plan   39
6   Section of Pine Decking from *Olympic*   43
7   Ticket for the Launch of *Titanic*   45
8   *Titanic* Coal   49
9   *Titanic* Lifeboat Plate   53
10 First Class Grand Staircase Bronze Cherub and Pedestal   57
11 First Class Staircase Cornice Moulding Section   60
12 Louis XV Dressing Table   62
13 Georgian Stateroom Door and Casing   64
14 First Class Bedstead   67
15 Turkish Bath Cooling Room Tiles   70
16 Swimming Bath Tile   73

Part III: *Titanic* Goes to Sea

17 Royal Naval Reserve Sword and Belt   79
18 Assistant Butcher Christopher Mills' Discharge
        Book and Pocket Watch   85

19 White Star Line Binoculars   87
20 White Star Line Officer's Hat   90
21 Shipyard Toolkit of Guarantee Group Member
        Artie Frost   98
22 White Star Line Third Class Ticket Book   100
23 Third Class Steward's Jacket   103
24 Letter Written by First Class Passenger Arthur Gee
        Aboard *Titanic*   109

Part IV: The Open Sea

25 White Star Line Deck Chair   123
26 First Class Dining Saloon Chair   126
27 Smoke Room Light Fixture   129
28 First Class Lounge Light Sconce   132
29 À La Carte Restaurant Receipt   135
30 Second Class Dining Room Chair   138
31 Turkish Bath Ticket   142
32 Blank Writing Paper with *Titanic* Letterhead
        and Envelope   145
33 'Honour and Glory Crowning Time'   149

Part V: Voyage into History

34 First Class Cut-Glass Electrolier   155
35 À La Carte Restaurant Serviette Ring   163
36 Quartermaster Alfred Olliver's Silver Pocket Watch   165
37 Period Ship's Wheel   169
38 Marconi Room Style Gimbal Lamp   174
39 White Star Line Lifeboat   178
40 Exterior Bulkhead Light   182
41 Bridge Megaphone from *Olympic*   191
42 Wallace Hartley's Sheet Music   193
43 Photo of Lifeboat No. 14 and Collapsible D   201
        Taken from *Carpathia*
44 Dickinson Letter, Written Aboard *Carpathia*   206
45 Spicer-Simson Medallion Commemorating
        Captain Rostron of *Carpathia*   214

46 White Star Line Paymaster's Uniform Jacket   219
47 British Wreck Commissioner's Inquiry and Report
        on the Loss of SS *Titanic*   221
48 Harland & Wolff Correspondence Concerning
        the Widows of Artie Frost, Robert Knight
        and Roderick Chisholm   225
49 First Paperback Edition of *A Night to Remember* (1956)   228
50 White Star Line Officer's Hat Used in the 1997
        Epic Film *Titanic*   231

Acknowledgements   233
References   235
Index   237

Foreword by Cathy Akers-Jordan

Titanic has been resting in her Atlantic grave for 110 years now, her bow standing upright as if still sailing, her stern an almost unidentifiable mess half a mile away. Bacteria are eating the iron, speeding the demise of the wreck. Already more decks are collapsing, and identifiable structures are losing their shapes.

While the fifty photographs collected in this book relate to *Titanic*, they are not from the actual wreck. They include unused items made for *Titanic*, some items that were carried off *Titanic* by passengers and some are similar items from her sister *Olympic*. They all have one thing in common: when gathered together, they represent the story of *Titanic* from the first imagining of the three *Olympic*-class sister ships to *Titanic*'s demise, researched and told by world-renowned *Titanic* experts Bruce Beveridge and Steve Hall. Both have published many books on *Titanic*, and I had the honour of working with them as part of the team who wrote *Report into the Loss of the SS Titanic: A Centennial Reappraisal* by Sam Halpern et al. (The History Press, 2012).

Bruce Beveridge is probably best known for the two-volume *Titanic: The Ship Magnificent*, written with Scott Andrews, Steve Hall, Daniel Klistorner and Art Braunschweiger. These books cover everything about *Titanic*, from her construction to her interior fittings, right down to the furniture placement on the deck plans. Beveridge also produced the extremely detailed deck plans in 36in x 54in poster form. For those seriously interested in *Titanic*'s technical specifications, these sources are invaluable.

Steve Hall has written many books about *Titanic*, but his favourite is *Titanic in Photographs*, written with Daniel Klistorner, Bruce Beveridge, Art Braunschweiger and Scott Andrews. Like *Titanic: The Ship Magnificent*, the collection of photos follows the life of *Titanic* from her birth in the shipyards of Harland & Wolff in Belfast, Ireland, to the aftermath of the disaster.

Titanic in 50 Objects is a fitting companion for the authors' previous works. Photos convey as much information, if not more, than written words. Photos are not abstract ideas but images of things we recognise and can relate to. For serious scholars, sometimes photos are the closest we can get to the actual event being studied. In other words, photos may be our only primary source.

Why study photos of everyday items instead of the latest forensic evidence? A few years ago, I was lucky enough to volunteer at a *Titanic* artefact exhibit. I spent my Saturdays strolling the exhibit and answering visitors' questions. The more time I spent with the artefacts (the cherub from the Grand Staircase, jewellery, money from almost every country in the world that survived in the purser's leather bag, personal toiletry items, clothing, china, crystal, dining utensils, bottles still containing olives or wine and pieces of *Titanic* herself, some twisted beyond recognition), the closer I felt to *Titanic* and her passengers.

Seeing these everyday items made the events even more real to me than James Cameron's film *Titanic*, where I first saw what she looked like in colour instead of black and white. These were real things used by real people; ordinary people, like you and me, and the extraordinarily rich and poor travelling in First and Third Class. Suddenly, those names became real people to me, so much so that I choked up when a visitor asked me about the band who played to the end.

Eventually, *Titanic* will decay to the point that she'll no longer be recognisable. All we'll have left of her will be pictures of her short life and her slow decay at the bottom of the ocean. Each picture is just one small part of *Titanic*'s story, a story to preserve while we can and to remember long afterwards.

Cathy Akers-Jordan, 2022

Author's Introduction

It has been 110 years since the *Titanic* collided with an iceberg in the North Atlantic and sank, taking with her some 1,500 lives. Since then, *Titanic*'s tragedy has been investigated to the nth degree; the story told over and over again, from documentaries to books and even in animated caricature. *Titanic* enthusiasts and historians, old and young alike, have at least one shelf dedicated to books on *Titanic* – and yet here is one more.

Steve and I had discussed a photo book even before *Titanic: The Ship Magnificent* was published in 2008. Finally, that idea took the form of *Titanic in Photographs*, with the primary author being Daniel Klistorner, and it was published in 2011. The rest of the writing team of Beveridge, Hall, Andrews and Braunschweiger worked with Daniel on this wonderful book, but afterwards, daily life had to take precedence over writing for all of us.

In 2014, Steve and I started putting together concepts for a book similar to *Titanic in Photographs*, but in this instance, with images of artefacts rather than archival photos. One challenge that we faced was finding artefacts from one collection. Since the 1997 release of James Cameron's film *Titanic*, the artefacts pertaining to *Titanic*, *Olympic* and the White Star Line have been generally scattered around the globe by way of auction and other forms of sale. Even to this day, the pertinent artefacts continue to scatter among the enthusiast community. I thank God for the sale at Jarrow of the fittings of the *Olympic* conducted by the auctioneers Knight, Frank & Rutley in 1935. If it weren't for them, and the buying of the 'Old Reliable's' fittings, I would have nothing to work from (nor would anyone else, for that matter).

The second challenge in the way of gathering artefact photos is the controversy over those items raised from the wreck site. This issue, compared by some to 'grave robbing', has drawn a rift between *Titanic* enthusiasts that is as severe as the legendary 'Hatfield's and McCoy's'. Steve and I preferred to stay neutral and

RMS *Olympic* arriving in New York Harbor, passing the Statue of Liberty. Just as her younger sister *Titanic* had a decade before, *Olympic*'s complement of immigrants had dreams of starting a new life in America. (Author's collection)

err on the safe side by choosing a collection that is not from the wreck site.

Lastly, whose collection do we gather images from? We have many friends who collect *Titanic*, *Olympic*, *Britannic* and White Star Line artefacts and memorabilia. I had approached a museum in the United States back in 2015 about using their items. I found that working with the museum's collection would be far too complex logistically, since they did not own some of the pieces I needed, but leased them from individual entities.

At the beginning of 2017, I was contracted to do consultation work on a new project that was very big in scope and expense. Steve was tapped once again to be my writing partner for a book to be written pertaining to the construction of the 'Unsinkable *Titanic*', the main attraction being built within the new Romandisea Resort located in Suning, China. Our book on artefact images was once again put on hold indefinitely, as this new project took precedence.

The research work needed to consult on the construction of the 'Unsinkable *Titanic*' brought me to England, along with my assistants, including Brian Thompson who later photographed the lifeboat for the cover of this book. My research team arrived in Southampton for the British Titanic Society Convention in April 2017.

It is here that I was greeted by old friends, whom I had not seen in some twenty years, and had the chance to finally meet David Scott-Beddard and John White for the first time in person. I had known the two of them for a number of years but had not met them face to face until that time. Their kindness was overwhelming; they are truly beautiful people and good friends.

John and David, along with fellow British Titanic Society officer Bob Angel, chaperoned my team throughout our needed history collecting tour of England, from the Maritime Museum in Liverpool, Kempton Steam Engine Museum in London and across Hadrian's Wall to the north. We continued on to the White Swan Hotel in Alnwick, England, where we researched and photographed *Olympic*'s First Class Lounge panelling in great detail. My European tour ended at White Star Memories' warehouse, where further analysis of David and John's collection took place.

In late summer 2017, I attended the grand opening of the White Star Memories exhibit '*Titanic* in Photographs', held on the *Queen Mary* in southern California. This was done in support of my friends David and John, as well as for research purposes, getting a deep behind-the-bulkheads tour of the 1930s-era ocean liner. The exhibit, with one of the last surviving White Star Line lifeboat as centre attraction, was a complete success. I will forever cherish the time I spent with David, John, Heidi and their exhibition crew, along with my team of Brian Thompson and Bill Young.

In 2018, the 'Unsinkable *Titanic*' attraction began to founder due to financing issues in Asia. The only event that year for which I am grateful is my marriage to Michele Murray – my best friend.

In 2020, Covid-19 halted everything – except the Beveridge and Hall artefact book that we had first discussed so many years before …

The call out for artefact photos went to David and John. White Star Memories holds a large number of relevant artefacts that were not raised from the wreck, and all in one place. (The exception being a large piece of coal that was retrieved from the debris field.)

Most of White Star Memories' collection is from *Olympic*. As any *Titanic* historian knows, the two ships were nearly identical and there are very few *Titanic*-specific pieces in existence. It is necessary to tell the story of *Titanic* with the help of *Olympic*. And as I have had to state a few times – the book is called *Titanic in 50 Objects*, not *Titanic in 50 Titanic Objects*!

While writing this book, and doing research on the passengers, I thought about those who are gone now – my fellow researchers, Roy Mengot and Larry Jibson. Now also Jack Eaton. Rest in Peace, my friends.

Bruce Beveridge
September 2022

PART I

THE OWNERS AND BUILDERS

1
White Star Line Advertising Brochure for *Olympic* and *Titanic*

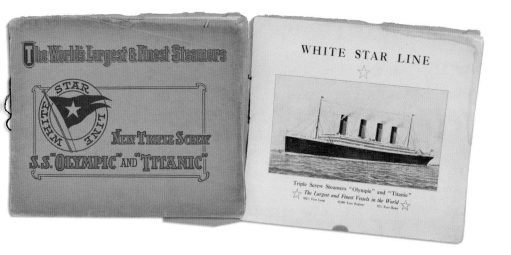

The White Star Line flag was originally the colours of a small line known primarily for its wooden sailing vessels. Thomas Henry Ismay bought the White Star Line and formed the Oceanic Steam Navigation Company on 6 September 1869, after a suggestion by, and support from, wealthy Liverpool businessman Gustavus C. Schwabe. The only condition to acquire Schwabe's financial support was that the managers of the new White Star Line must purchase all of their ships from Harland & Wolff, a shipbuilding firm of Belfast, Ireland, of which Schwabe's nephew, Gustav Wolff, was a junior partner.

Thomas Ismay.
(Author's
collection)

Ismay had some knowledge of iron ships and the Atlantic traffic because he was once the director of the National Line. He recognised the advantages of a high class of steamships. He was joined in 1870 by William Imrie, a good friend of his (they had apprenticed together), and together they created the management firm of Ismay, Imrie & Co.

An order was immediately placed with Harland & Wolff to begin the construction of a new fleet of ships. In August 1870, the first vessel launched at the Queen's Island yard was the first *Oceanic*. She arrived in the Mersey in February 1871. The ship was 420ft long, 41ft broad, and 31ft deep, with a tonnage of 3,707. *Oceanic* embodied a number of improvements seen for the first time in the Atlantic trade. A four-cylinder compound engine propelled her, giving a speed of about 14 knots, with a coal consumption of 65 tons per day.

White Star
Line's RMS
Oceanic, 1899.
(Author's
collection)

Following the first *Oceanic* came a long list of notable liners. The first, *Britannic* (I), was built in 1874, and *Germanic* followed in 1875. These vessels had an increased speed over *Oceanic* (I) and were capable of obtaining over 16 knots. This fact greatly reduced the time of transatlantic passage to less than seven and a half days.

In August 1896, *Germanic* accomplished the journey in six days and twenty-one hours. This was the last attempt for speed the White Star Line made until 1889, when *Teutonic* and *Majestic* (I) were put into service.

J. Bruce Ismay, the eldest son of Thomas Ismay, was born in 1862. On 13 September 1880, he entered the firm of Ismay, Imrie & Co. to serve his apprenticeship. On 21 January 1886, he sailed aboard *Celtic* (I) from Liverpool to take up his new appointment as an agent for the White Star Line in New York.

It was in New York that Bruce met Harold Arthur Sanderson, who was employed by Wilson & Company. Theirs was a friendship that would last for many years. Ismay took leave to travel back to Liverpool with his wife and six-month-old daughter at the request of his father, who, on 1 January 1891, admitted Bruce as a partner.

In 1899 the second *Oceanic* was completed. This ship exceeded the dimensions of any liner to this date and was the first to exceed

J. Bruce Ismay.
(Author's
collection)

the length of *Great Eastern*, which was the largest ship in the world up until that time.

The greatness of the new *Oceanic* also symbolised the end of an era. Thomas Ismay was diagnosed with gallstones and became so ill that he could not attend the sea trials of *Oceanic* on 25 August 1899. Bruce was dispatched to attend the event on his own. However, the elder Ismay insisted on being taken aboard the tender *Magnetic* so that he could meet *Oceanic* as she arrived at the Mersey.

On 23 November 1899, Thomas Ismay passed away in his home, with his wife, Margaret, at his side. At the age of 37, Bruce Ismay had now achieved his ambition of succeeding his father as chairman of the White Star Line.

White Star returned to the slower but larger vessels with the completion of the second *Celtic* of 1903, the first of the 'Big Four', which also included *Cedric*, *Baltic* and *Adriatic*. However, Ismay decided to take a new approach to the Atlantic trade. He determined that it would be best for the White Star Line to concentrate on size and luxury, but with enough speed to transport passengers across the Atlantic in a competitive amount of time; competing for the coveted Blue Riband was left to other ship companies. The faster ships consumed great quantities of coal for a small amount of extra speed with added engine vibration.

J. Piermont Morgan. (Author's collection)

International Mercantile Marine

The American financier J. Pierpont Morgan formed International Mercantile Marine (IMM) on 1 October 1902. Morgan had control of the railroads carrying goods in the United States, but not the shipping that brought over imported goods. Morgan wanted to control both. Being an American citizen, Morgan could not own British ships, but he could own a company which then owned British ships.

IMM was bankrolled by Morgan and J.P. Morgan & Co., but it was directed by shipping magnates Clement Griscom, of the American Line and Red Star Line; Bernard N. Baker, of the Atlantic Transport Line;

RMS *Mauretania* was built by Swan Hunter for the Cunard Line. Launched on 20 September 1906, she was the world's largest ship until the launch of RMS *Olympic* in 1910. (Author's collection)

J. Bruce Ismay, of the White Star Line; and John Ellerman, of the Leyland Line.

The Dominion Line fell under the control of IMM, which also had profit-sharing relationships with the German Hamburg-America and the North German Lloyd lines. IMM was a holding company that controlled the various shipping lines listed above as subsidiary corporations, but it was also a trust. Eight of the thirteen directors of IMM were American, and the remaining five were British.

With the agreement to join IMM, Bruce Ismay would remain as the Managing Director of the White Star Line. Its ships retained their British registries and were manned by British crews.

As a result of the formation of IMM, the British Government arranged to loan the Cunard line, White Star's top competitor, the necessary capital for the building of two new fast steamers, as well as a yearly subsidy of £150,000 for twenty years. In exchange, these vessels would be available as Royal Naval auxiliaries in time of war. In 1905, Cunard contracted with John Brown & Co. Ltd, of Clydebank, and Swan, Hunter & Wigham Richardson Ltd, of Wallsend on Tyne, to build their two new express steamers, *Lusitania* and *Mauretania*.

The design requirements imposed were such as to ensure they surpassed anything the world had ever seen in terms of size and speed. The two ships were about 790ft long and approximately 32,000 gross registered tons each. Both ships were launched in 1906 and began commercial service in 1907.

Cunard's RMS *Lusitania* launched on 7 June 1906. Although significantly faster than the *Olympic* class would be, the speed and port turnaround times of Cunard's vessels were not sufficient to allow the line to run a weekly two-ship transatlantic service from each side of the ocean. (Author's collection)

2

Harland & Wolff Builder's Plate

Posted in pertinent locations around the decks of every ship constructed by Harland & Wolff were builder's plates. In most cases, these would be seen on a bulkhead in the Engine Room and at a prominent position on the Weather Deck. In the case of *Titanic*, a plate was located in the Reciprocating Engine Room and on the centreline of the exterior athwartship plating of B Deck forward. The pictured example is a later version of the style used in 1910.

By the beginning of the twentieth century, several British firms had become world leaders in shipbuilding. Swan, Hunter & Wigham Richardson Ltd of Wallsend on Tyne, for example, was

the builder of *Mauretania* and a significant number of other ships of the Cunard fleet. Another of Cunard's preferred builders, John Brown & Co., of Clydebank, built *Lusitania*.

Harland & Wolff, of Belfast, enjoyed a particularly close association with the White Star Line, being the exclusive builder for ships launched under the White Star name. *Titanic*'s launch in 1911 gave Harland & Wolff the distinction of having produced a greater aggregate tonnage in one year than any other shipyard in the world. But what made Harland & Wolff stand apart from most yards was the fact that it was equipped to completely design, build and launch a ship – hull, machinery, interiors, furnishings – all at its own works. Thus, when White Star decided to build the *Olympic*-class ships, it had full confidence that Harland & Wolff could deliver.

Harland & Wolff was started by Edward J. Harland in 1859, when he acquired the shipyard of his former employer, Robert Hickson & Co. He was joined by Gustav W. Wolff in 1861, and in January of 1862, the company's name was officially changed to Harland & Wolff to reflect the new partnership. In 1874, three

(Left to right) Gustav Wolff, W.H. Wilson, William J. Pirrie and Edward Harland. (Author's collection)

others were taken into the partnership – William J. Pirrie, Walter H. Wilson and Alexander B. Wilson.

Alexander Wilson retired shortly after joining the firm, Sir Edward Harland died in 1895 and Gustav Wolff retired from the firm in 1903, after selling his shares in the partnership to Pirrie. With the death of Walter Wilson in 1904, William J. Pirrie – known as Lord Pirrie after being elevated to the peerage in 1906 – remained as the chairman and sole principal in the business.

Under Lord Pirrie, there were six managing directors, each being responsible for the day-to-day operations of one particular department. These directors were the Right Honourable Alexander M. Carlisle, Chairman of the Managing Directors and Chief Naval Architect; W.J. Pratten, Consulting Engineer (Pratten had only just retired as Manager of the Engine Works); John W. Kempster, Manager of the Electrical Department; Thomas Andrews, Head of the Design Department; George Cuming, Engine Works Manager and Robert Crighton, Manager of the Harland & Wolff works at Southampton. Naval Architect Edward Wilding, who was responsible for all critical design calculations, reported directly to Thomas Andrews.

PART II

TITANIC CONCEIVED

3
White Star Line Advertising Brochure

The White Star Line issued brochures with the anticipated sailing schedules of their two new super-sized ocean liners before they were completed. This was to get public interest spurred in preparation for the commercial service of *Olympic* and *Titanic*.

Three new ships were conceived by Bruce Ismay and Lord Pirrie prior to April 1907. These were the sisters *Olympic*, *Titanic* and, later, *Britannic*. Once all three *Olympic*-class liners were in service, they could easily maintain a weekly service out of New York and Southampton. The *Mauretania* and *Lusitania* were not quick enough to operate a two-ship weekly return service from New York, so the additional 4 or 5 knots of speed that the Cunard ships had over White Star was to prove to no great advantage. Although many passengers enjoyed travelling on the fastest ships, the White Star Line had an unassailable position in size, luxury and safety over their Cunard competitors.

Olympic and *Titanic* were to be part of a fleet of thirteen ships employed in the transport of passengers and cargo between Great Britain and the United States. This included mail, which gave them the designation of RMS – 'Royal Mail Steamer'. The usual ports of call for the service would be Southampton, Cherbourg, Plymouth, Queenstown and New York.

The White Star Line was already operating a weekly trans-atlantic service between Southampton and New York, with the 21-knot *Oceanic*, 17-knot *Adriatic* and the two 20-knot liners *Teutonic* and *Majestic*. It was planned that when *Olympic* entered service she would replace *Adriatic* and *Titanic* would replace *Majestic*. *Oceanic* would operate with *Olympic* and *Titanic* until *Britannic* was in service. When *Britannic* took over the transatlantic route, *Oceanic* would then be transferred to other service, but would be placed back in transatlantic service when an overhaul of any of the *Olympic*-class liners required temporary removal.

Britannic was not added to the fleet until the summer of 1914. When completed, the three ships registered in at approximately 45,500 gross tons each (*Britannic* would later register at about 50,000 tons) and measured 882ft 9in long and 92ft 6in wide at the maximum breadth of the ship. As a comparison to later ships, the German-registered *Imperator* (1913) was 909ft long and *Queen Mary* (1936) was just over 1,000ft.

White Star's plan was to eclipse the Cunard Line's *Mauretania* and *Lusitania* in both luxury and size, but to design and build a trio of ships of such unprecedented scale was no small task. Coincidently, Harland & Wolff had in place both the technical expertise and the shipbuilding facilities to handle just such a project. By 1910, Harland & Wolff Ltd was a full-service company employing some 14,000 men, including both subcontractors and 'on-site' personnel. Approximately 6,000 of those would be

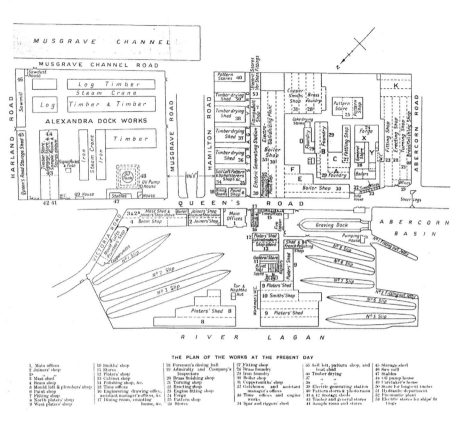

THE PLAN OF THE WORKS AT THE PRESENT DAY

1. Main offices
2. Joiners' shop
2a. " "
3. Mast shed
4. Beam shop
5. Mould loft & plumbers' shop
6. Paint shop
7. Fitting shop
8. North platers' shop
9. West platers' shop
10. Smiths' shop
11. Stores
12. Platers' shop
13. Cabinet shop
14. Polishing shop, &c.
15. Time offices
16. Engineering drawing-office, assistant manager's offices, &c.
17. Dining room, counting house, &c.
18. Foremen's dining hall
19. Admiralty and Company's Inspectors
20. Brass finishing shop
21. Turning shop
22. Erecting shop
23. Engine fitting shop
24. Forge
25. Pattern shop
26. Stores
27. Fitting shop
28. Brass foundry
29. Iron foundry
30. Boiler shop
31. Coppersmiths' shop
32. Gatehouse and assistant manager's offices
33. Time offices and engine works
34. Spar and riggers' shed
35. Sail loft, pattern shop, and boat shed
36. Timber drying
37. " "
38. " "
39. Electric generating station
40. Pattern stores & photo room
41 & 42. Storage sheds
43. Timber and general stores
44. Sample room and stores
45. Storage shed
46. Saw mill
47. Stables
48. Oil pump house
49. Caretaker's home
50. Store for longest timber
51. Hydraulic department
52. Pneumatic plant
53. Electric stores for ships' fittings

involved with the building of *Olympic* and *Titanic*, with approximately 1,000 working on the nightshift.

The Belfast facility at Queen's Island contained no less than eight building slips, all capable of accommodating large vessels. However, due to the enormous size of the two new vessels, the berths in which *Olympic* and *Titanic* were built – Slips 2 and 3 – were constructed on an area previously occupied by three slips.

Even though Pirrie and Ismay envisioned the *Olympic*-class liners, the actual design work was undertaken by the shipyard's principal architect, Alexander Carlisle. Thomas Andrews was head of the yard's design department and oversaw the creation of the class prototype plans, but Carlisle took charge of the details. Throughout all of the stages of design and planning, all drawings and specifications were submitted to Ismay for his approval. Any

Plan of the Harland & Wolff yards as they appeared in 1911. (Author's collection)

modifications or suggestions he believed necessary were without doubt carried out. History tells us that all his later suggestions were aesthetically based.

Alexander Carlisle resigned from Harland & Wolff in 1911 and took a position with the Welin Davit Company, which manufactured and supplied the lifeboat davits for *Olympic* and *Titanic*. Though there has been much speculation as to why Carlisle resigned, nothing has been verified about his true intentions for leaving.

4

Rivets from the Construction Berths of *Titanic* and *Olympic*

These two unused rivets were retrieved from the construction berths of *Olympic* and *Titanic*. Henry Solomon was a 'holder on' in a riveting squad that constructed *Titanic*. Henry, who had worked at the yard along with his father William, brought these rivets home as souvenirs of the largest ships in the world.

Design work commenced on *Olympic* and *Titanic* following the 'Order to Proceed' filed on 30 April 1907. The basic hull lines and the layout of propelling machinery was decided early in the process and, after numerous preliminary iterations, approval of the overall initial design by White Star directors followed on 29 July 1908.

Harland & Wolff was given orders to proceed with the actual construction of *Olympic* (Yard No. 400) and *Titanic* (Yard No. 401) on 17 September 1908. As ship names were only used officially by the builder after the ships were launched, most plans and specifications provided for the construction were titled by yard numbers only.

Construction began with the ordering of parts. As construction on 401 was to begin shortly after the start of 400, many of the fittings were ordered at the same time. This included the interior woodwork, furniture and other decorations, as well as the steel and iron needed for the construction of the hulls.

All of the required parts had to be ready for fabrication or installation, and the shops at Harland & Wolff began to work on upcoming projects as soon as possible without regard to whether the items were needed immediately or not. Work began on fittings such as doors, hatches and manholes as soon as the plans became available, thereby providing work for the Blacksmith, Pattern, Foundry, Machine and Galvanising Shops. The completed fittings would then be stored until required.

Since the first two of the three planned *Olympic*-class ships would be built simultaneously, they would share many of the same construction plans. As construction progressed on *Olympic*, any changes decided upon for *Titanic* were indicated by notes written on the plans, listing the hull number to which they applied; in instances where the differences were considerable, separate drawings were made for *Titanic*.

Work on the construction of Yard No. 400 commenced on 16 December 1908 with the laying of her keel. A few weeks later, it was completed using hydraulic riveting wherever possible. The seams of the ship's bottom hull plating were double riveted (two parallel rows of rivets where two shell plates met), whereas the topside hull plating had been triple and quadruple riveted for extra strength.

On 22 March 1909, construction work on Yard No. 401 officially commenced with the placement and positioning of the keel blocks on the new slipway. Over a week later, on Wednesday,

31 March 1909, the first piece of keel plate was placed on the blocks. *Titanic* was fully plated to her double bottom by 15 May of the same year, but thereafter, progress of her construction began to lag and the various stages of construction were accomplished at a slower pace than those of her sister. The largest factor in the lag time between the progress of 400 and 401 was the logistics involved in manufacturing the massive steel castings.

Titanic's rudder, stern frame and boss arm brackets for the wing propellers were designed by Harland & Wolff, but the manufacturing of the enormous castings was entrusted to the Darlington Forge Company, an outside firm located in England. The castings were all of Siemens–Martin mild cast steel, with the exception of the rudder stock, which was of forged ingot steel.

The making of the moulds in which the stern frame was cast represented two months' work. Another five months were required for the completion of the finished castings, for a total of seven months' time. In casting the pieces making up the stern frame alone, about 95 tons of molten steel were required, the finished

The construction berths of *Olympic* and *Titanic*. (Author's collection)

The after-shaft brackets of *Titanic* in the shop before being taken to the construction slip. Here, the port and starboard halves have been temporarily assembled for machining of the attachments to the hull. (Author's collection)

weight of these pieces being some 70 tons. Not unexpectedly, construction of 401 was also delayed due to problems in delivering some of these large steel castings from Darlington Forge.

By late November of 1909, all but the last of *Olympic*'s frames had been raised into position and the framing of *Titanic* had progressed sufficiently that on 21 December, Harland & Wolff took delivery of a number of the steel castings from Darlington Forge. These included the stern frame and stern shaft brackets for *Titanic* as well as the rudder for *Olympic*; the largest ever produced for any ship.

The Darlington Forge Company had to make special arrangements with the local railway as one of the castings extended 14ft beyond the side of the railway tracks, requiring heavy balance weights to be placed on the opposite side. The operation was carried out with great care, and the train, which never travelled faster than 4mph, eventually delivered the castings to Hartlepool where they were placed aboard the Antrim Iron Ore Company's steamer *Glenravel* for delivery to Belfast.

On Wednesday, 23 March 1910, J. Bruce Ismay visited Harland & Wolff and inspected the building of *Olympic* and *Titanic*. By this stage, *Olympic* was almost fully plated and *Titanic* was only two weeks away from having her last frame put into position. This is the only time that Ismay is known to have visited Harland & Wolff to inspect the ships' construction, except for when they were launched.

The visit was of an official capacity, and it was on this occasion that an important conference took place between Ismay, Lord Pirrie, Alexander Carlisle, Harold Sanderson and other leading officials of the White Star Line. The group no doubt discussed many aspects of the ships' construction, design and decoration of passenger accommodations. Discussions also included safety provisions for the two ships, where Alexander Carlisle's proposal of lifeboats for all on board was turned down.

By 15 April 1910, *Olympic* was fully plated and by early July, significant progress was being made in the plating of *Titanic*. *Olympic*'s launch was announced to take place on 20 October and preparations for the launch were well in hand. With the impending launch and the expected completion of *Olympic* by the summer of 1911, a new Ocean Dock was being constructed in Southampton because no other dock was large enough for berthing the two huge liners.

In New York, negotiations with the Harbor Commission continued regarding the extension of the Chelsea Piers into the Hudson River. Additional dredging of both the Ambrose Channel and around the Chelsea Piers continued to increase the depth of water in order to permit the passage of the new class of ships at all tides.

In Cherbourg, there was no pier large enough nor dock deep enough to allow the berthing of the new liners. Therefore, in October 1910, the White Star Line placed an order for two new tenders, *Nomadic* and *Traffic*, to be used to ferry passengers, baggage and mails to the ships, which would be anchored outside the breakwater.

By February 1911, *Titanic* was at a stage of construction where it was apparent she would soon be ready for launch. On 27 February, *Titanic*'s huge 101¼-ton rudder (which had been cast as six separate pieces) arrived at Harland & Wolff, having been dispatched by the Darlington Forge Company. The rudder arrived on the steamer *Glenravel*, much as *Titanic*'s stern frame and *Olympic*'s rudder had in December 1909.

While *Titanic*'s intended launch date of 31 May 1911 was already being circulated as early as December 1910, Harland & Wolff did not officially announce this date until 7 March 1911. On Sunday, 30 April 1911, *Titanic*'s centre anchor and two side anchors, manufactured by Noah Hingley & Sons, were dispatched to Dudley, where they were loaded onto a special train and made their way to the Fleetwood shipping docks. Other equipment such as chains, cables and attachments were delivered to Fleetwood in the following days, and everything was finally delivered to Harland & Wolff on Friday, 5 May aboard the *Duke of Albany*. At some point later in May, *Titanic*'s hull was painted in preparation for launch and the anchors were fitted shortly thereafter.

It was written in *The Shipbuilder* magazine that there were 500,000 rivets in *Titanic*'s double bottom alone, the aggregate weight of the rivets being about 270 tons, with the largest rivets being 1¼in in diameter. There were about 3 million rivets throughout the entire ship, weighing approximately 1,200 tons. An interesting point is that riveters were paid by the rivet, not by the hour, and Harland & Wolff's payroll included 'rivet counters'. *Titanic* was built with two types of rivets: wrought iron and steel. The wrought-iron rivets were closed by hand; the steel rivets were closed by hydraulic riveting machines and placed within the hull at points where extra strength was needed.

5

No. 401 – *Titanic*'s Rigging Plan

This copy of the original Harland & Wolff Rigging Plan is one of the few builder's plans that actually addressed the ship by name as well as yard number: No. 401 – *Titanic*. The 1/144 scale profile was created in Harland & Wolff's Drawing Office by a team of draftsmen who drew the plans by hand, using pencil on linen. The prints that are often seen with white lines on a blue background are copies of the original created using a photosensitive chemical process.

Draughtsmen working on the design drawings of a ship in the Harland & Wolff Drawing Office, around 1910. (Author's collection)

Most of the plans for *Titanic* and *Olympic* were drawn at 1/48 scale, also known as ¼in = 1ft. For a ship 882.9ft in length, it is easy to see how some of the construction plans extended to over 18ft in length. In order to copy a drawing of that size, the draftsmen at Harland & Wolff would lay the original plan and copying medium on a large tray then roll the whole of it out of a window to be exposed to the sun for a predetermined amount of time. The special chemical used reacted to UV light and turned the copy medium the blue colour, while the pencil lines on the original were opaque and did not allow light through. Simply explained, the plan seen on the previous page is a negative of the original.

The Rigging Plan held a lot of general information, including the ship's paint scheme (livery), the diameter of the permanent rigging and shrouds that held the masts and funnels in place, the height of the masts and the location of the navigational lights. A copy of the Rigging Plan was stored on *Titanic*'s bridge.* For the *Titanic* enthusiast, the Rigging Plan is an invaluable reference.

---

*   (Along with other pertinent plans needed by the deck officers. The need for this plan is probably why the ship's name is used on the drawing, along with 401.)

The *Olympic*-class liners were the first to be designed with a 'yacht-like' profile, as it was described. Ships of this era had large amounts of ventilation heads, skylights and other equipment cluttering the weather decks. Augmenting the clutter, ships would also have 'island' deckhouses, divided with large spaces between them to give access to cargo hatches. *Titanic*'s design and size allowed for access to the cargo holds fore and aft of the superstructure, leaving it unbroken in profile. Furthermore, Harland & Wolff used electric motor-assisted ventilation as much as possible to eliminate large numbers of the trumpet-shaped ventilation heads. *Titanic* was a beautiful ship with her unbroken lines – truly yacht-like.

Titanic's builder's specifications:

Hull number	401
Length overall	882ft 9in
Length between perpendiculars	850ft 0in
Breadth extreme	92ft 6in
Depth moulded to Shelter Deck	64ft 3in
Depth moulded to Bridge Deck	73ft 3in
Total height from keel to Navigating Bridge	104ft 0in
Load draft upon completion	34ft 7in

Titanic was designed with a 'schooner' rig, straight stem and a graceful, elliptical counter stern. She had four funnels and two masts and was classed by the Board of Trade as a 'shelter deck vessel'. *Titanic* was built to adhere to the regulations of the United Kingdom and the United States for both passenger and immigrant ships.

Titanic's two pole masts were spaced about 600ft apart. These masts were made of steel, except for a 15ft teak section at the top. The masts stood approximately 205ft above the maximum load line, a height necessary to accommodate the Marconi aerial wires. This ensured that, at its lowest point, the aerial would be at least 35ft above the top of the funnels and away from constant contact with the corrosive funnel gases.

One of the most visible features of *Titanic* was her four massive funnels. Each funnel was 24ft × 19ft in diameter, but they were not all the same height. The forward funnel (No. 1) stood 70ft above the level of the Boat Deck; No. 2 and No. 3 funnels stood 74ft; and No. 4 funnel stood 73ft above the Boat Deck.

The first three funnels were utilised to vent combustion gases from the boilers, with the fourth being called a 'dummy', although it was actually designed to function as a ventilator. This dummy funnel was also intended to enhance and give balance to the profile of the ship. At the same time, it also gave the impression of greater power and speed to those non-technical passengers who tended to judge and compare vessels by the number of funnels they carried.

6

Section of Pine Decking
from *Olympic*

This section of 3in-thick pitch pine wood decking from *Olympic* was cut from a larger lot that was bought at auction in 1935.

Titanic used two types of pine for her deck planking. Yellow pine was used throughout, except in areas that would undergo excessive wear; these latter surfaces were laid with pitch pine. Pitch pine is distinguished from yellow pine by its peculiarly rough, dark

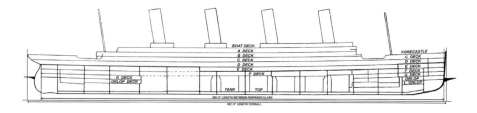

Profile plan
of *Titanic*.
(Author's
collection)

bark, and its abundance of resin. The planking which bordered
the sides of the decks and around the deckhouses was teak.

Titanic had miles of wood decking on her weather decks and
below in certain areas subject to excessive moisture or wear, such
as in the working passageway on E Deck. A two-storey timber
drying shed was included in the Harland & Wolff works, where
the deck planking was dried, along with the many types of wood
used for ship construction and in the manufacturing shops.

Titanic had eight passenger decks, consisting of the Boat Deck,
Promenade Deck (A), Bridge Deck (B), Shelter Deck (C), Saloon
Deck (D), Upper Deck (E), Middle Deck (F), and Lower Deck
(G), while at each end of the ship there was a partial deck known
as the Orlop Deck. The after end of the Orlop Deck aft of WTB
(Watertight Bulkhead) 'O' and immediately above the after-shaft
tunnels was also referred to on the main structural drawings as
the 'Tunnel Deck'. This portion of the deck was designed to create
a watertight flat above the after-shaft tunnel in order to prevent
flooding of the hold above in the event of a complete failure of
any of the tailshafts or stern tubes. There was also an additional
deck located forward within the No. 1 Hold, called the Lower
Orlop Deck.

At the very lowest level within the ship, the top plating of the
double bottom was called the 'Tank Top'. These last three levels
were not considered decks in the formal sense of the term and,
in many publications dealing with the *Olympic*-class ships, are
often omitted when the various decks are described. This meant
that although *Titanic* had eight 'passenger' decks, there were actually eleven deck levels in total, not counting certain areas of the
superstructure referred to by some seamen as 'sun decks' and
'fiddley decks'.

7
Ticket for the Launch of *Titanic*

Titanic towered overhead in the gantry as more than 100,000 people turned out to witness the events of the day. Those nearby walked, while cars, taxis and trolleys conveyed spectators to the yard. To accommodate those fortunate enough to attend, Harland & Wolff provided a number of viewing locations. On the opposite side of the river to where *Titanic* waited in her slipway, a section of grounds had been railed off, for which a charge of admission was made to purchase a ticket, with the proceeds given to various Belfast hospitals.

The White Star Line benefitted from a fortunate coincidence in timing when *Titanic* was ready for launch on 31 May 1911 – it was the same day that *Olympic* returned from her sea trials prior to her final departure from Belfast.

Dressed in holiday attire, J. Bruce Ismay, J.P. Morgan and other distinguished guests travelled to Belfast in the chartered ferry *Duke of Argyll* to attend. A significant number of guests and representatives from the press were accommodated on a large stand directly facing the stern of *Titanic*, while the best seats for special guests of the owners and builders were on a stand constructed near the port bow.

After the last of the supporting shores had been removed, *Titanic* was left resting solely on the fore and aft poppets on the sliding ways. To lubricate the slipway and reduce the friction on the ways, some 15 tons of tallow and 3 tons of train oil mixed with 3 tons of soft soap were used.

Seconds after the launch triggers had been released at 12.13 p.m., the hull gracefully slid stern first into the river. Drag chains and steel hawsers with anchors had been used to arrest the backward movement of the massive hull and bring it to a standstill once afloat. Celebratory whistles echoed through the Belfast air from ships witnessing the event as the vessel settled gracefully into the water, and small craft from the shipyard collected the flotsam from the launch cradle.

As was customary for White Star Ships, there was no launch ceremony with the usual bottle of champagne broken over the bow. Harland & Wolff merely fired rockets to give warning for vessels in the river to stand clear, and with the release of the launching trigger – a huge hydraulic ram that initiated the initial push – the hull slid down the way into the water. At 12.15 p.m., *Titanic* was afloat and clear of the gantry. Following the launch, the yard workers proceeded to detach the metal hawsers from the river anchors and drag chains.

With the festivities completed, the dignitaries and their guests withdrew to the Grand Central Hotel in Belfast while Lord Pirrie's party stayed at Queen's Island. Later, the dignitaries were taken aboard the new tender *Nomadic* to *Olympic*, which departed at 4.15 p.m. for Liverpool, her first stop before going to Southampton where she would commence her maiden voyage.

Titanic's launch, 31 May 1911. (Author's collection)

Titanic was taken in tow to the Fitting-Out Wharf, located at some distance from the main shipyard. To bring all the heavy machinery from the shops to the ship's new location, Harland & Wolff operated a steam tram with small rail trucks. Everything that would be put aboard the ship from this point forward – boilers, funnels, engine bedplates, turbines, condensers and other equipment and fittings – would be brought by rail. An extensive network of rail lines ran throughout the yard and terminated at the Fitting-Out Wharf.

To transfer all of the heavy equipment and machinery from the rail trucks into the ship, Harland & Wolff purchased a 200-ton floating crane with a maximum lifting weight of 150 tons, a lifting height of 150ft, and a loading radius of 100ft. The crane also had a smaller cable-operated hook capable of lifting 50 tons.

Work on *Titanic* continued apace until 6 October 1911, when *Olympic* returned for unforeseen and extensive repairs. This required a large percentage of the workforce to be shifted from *Titanic* to her sister, and while work did continue on *Titanic*, her progress was delayed. As a consequence, the White Star Line was forced to reschedule her maiden voyage from 20 March 1912 to 10 April.

Titanic at the fitting-out wharf used by Harland & Wolff to undergo the final stages of construction. It is here that such components as the engines, boilers, funnels and the interior fittings were brought aboard. (Author's collection)

By January 1912, *Titanic* had all four of her funnels in place. The boilers and heavy machinery had been lowered into the hull some time before. She was now ready for the dry dock to accommodate the installation of her three massive propellers and the painting of her lower hull.

When *Titanic* entered the huge dry dock on 3 February 1912, the event was captured in a short two-minute newsreel. That film is, to this day, the only known moving picture taken of the ship.

Two weeks later, on 17 February, the necessary work in the dry dock was completed and she was removed and shifted back to the fitting-out wharf.

8

Titanic Coal

Among the debris scattered around the ocean floor at *Titanic*'s wreck site are huge chunks of coal. A number of *Titanic*'s coal bunkers emptied their contents as the hull broke in half during the 2½-mile descent to the bottom. This large piece of coal was raised from the debris field during a past dive to *Titanic*'s final resting place.

The steam required to power all of *Titanic*'s machinery was provided by twenty-nine huge boilers that comprised 159 furnaces. There were twenty-four double-ended boilers and five single-ended boilers. To feed these massive boilers, the ship's coal bunkers had a combined capacity of 6,611 tons and, operating at

21–22 knots, could consume 620–640 tons of coal per day, all hand fed by shovel. A further 1,092 tons of coal could be shipped in the reserve bunker hold forward of Boiler Room No. 6.

The reciprocating engines were of the four-cylinder, triple-expansion, direct-acting inverted type configuration with a high, an intermediate, and two low-pressure cylinders. Each of these engines developed 15,000 IHP (indicated horsepower) at 75 rpm. The low-pressure turbine developed around 16,000 SHP (shaft horsepower) at 165 rpm. The exhaust steam drove this centre turbine from the two reciprocating engines. This impressive array of machinery was capable of generating up to 51,000 horsepower combined, giving the ship a service speed of 21–21½ knots. However, the maximum speed was believed to be 24 knots.

Titanic was driven by a triple-screw arrangement. The two giant reciprocating engines drove her port and starboard wing propellers, while the low-pressure turbine drove the centreline shaft. Because the turbine was not equipped to move in 'reverse', the centre propeller operated only in the 'ahead' direction.

Safety Provisions and Equipment

A 1911 *Shipbuilder* magazine article, describing the construction of *Titanic* and *Olympic*, stated that when the watertight doors were closed, the ship would be 'practically unsinkable'. However, one will be hard pressed to find this term used as blatantly as it was for Cunard's *Mauretania* and *Lusitania*. This bold statement was based on the watertight compartments within the hulls of these ships. Unfortunately, the 'practically unsinkable' description has been attached to *Titanic* as if the White Star Line created it for the first time in history, just to lure in unsuspecting customers.

The definition of the 'unsinkable ship' had been argued long before *Titanic*. As one example, Cunard's *Saxonia* of 1900 was called 'practically unsinkable' because of her transverse and longitudinal watertight bulkheads. Similar publicity was presented in 1903 with the Hamburg-America liner *Deutschland*, which was fitted with watertight bulkheads and the use of the newly

Opposite: One of *Titanic*'s huge four-storey-high engines in the Construction Shed at Harland & Wolff. (Author's collection)

patented Stone-Lloyd hydraulically controlled marine safety bulkhead doors.

Titanic's main transverse bulkheads were made watertight, thus subdividing the vessel into watertight compartments so that, in the event of damage, any flooding could be contained. All doors through these bulkheads, which were designed to be watertight, were fitted with gaskets and were kept clear at all times so that they could be closed at a moment's notice.

The watertight subdivision of *Titanic* was considered very comprehensive at the time of her building. The design was such that any two main compartments could be flooded with the ship loaded to the maximum load draft without affecting the safety of the ship. The minimum freeboard the vessel would have in the event of any two compartments being flooded was between 2ft 6in and 8ft from the deck adjoining the top of the watertight bulkheads (known as the 'Bulkhead Deck'). In *Titanic*, any three of the four forward compartments could have been flooded to the top of her lowest watertight bulkhead without sinking the ship.

The ship would remain afloat even with the four forward compartments flooded in a relatively calm sea. However, in heavy seas, the water could run along the decks aft of the forward bulkheads, finding its way below into the fifth compartment aft through the various non-watertight openings within the decks. Even in this state, the survival of the ship would still be possible, providing the rate of flooding was not beyond the capabilities of the bilge pumps.

9

Titanic Lifeboat Plate

Various metal identification plates were attached to the exterior of Titanic's 30ft and 25f lifeboats. At the forward and after ends, a name plate with raised letters 'S.S. Titanic' was applied to the outboard side and the port of registry, 'Liverpool', was applied on the inboard side of the boats. These words were cast into brass plates 15in long. White Star Line flag plates were also applied forward and aft on both sides, and draft plates with 7/8in lettering identifying length, breadth, depth and capacity were applied to the forward inboard side.

The sixteen boats were assigned numbers according to their position on deck identified by metal boat numbers applied to the forward and after ends, port and starboard, 2½–3in in height. Starboard boats were odd numbered and port boats were even numbered. The numbering started with the forwardmost starboard boat, which was No. 1, and the forward-most port boat as No. 2, from here, the numbering continued, alternating from starboard to port and proceeding aft.

Titanic had fourteen 30ft boats with a combined capacity of 910 persons, and two smaller 25ft emergency cutters with a combined capacity of eighty persons. The cutters were rigged under the foremost davits near the bridge and were kept permanently swung out while at sea so that they could be lowered quickly if needed. It was quite common for large vessels, steaming in excess of 20 knots, to

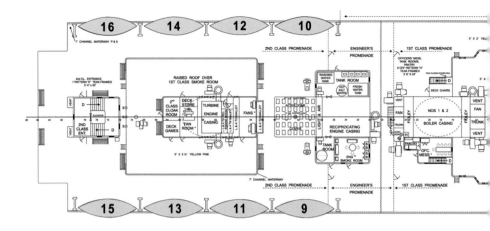

Plan of *Titanic*'s Boat Deck, showing the numbering of the lifeboats. (Author's collection)

collide with fishing boats on the Grand Banks off Newfoundland, and the cutters also had to be kept in readiness in case someone fell overboard.

Titanic was also equipped with an additional four 27ft 5in-long Engelhardt collapsible boats with a combined capacity of 188 people. The collapsibles were so named because they had wooden bottoms and adjustable canvas sides that could be pulled up and snapped taut by means of hinged steel braces.

Two of the collapsibles were secured to the deck beneath the emergency cutters and the remaining two were secured to the roof of the Officers' Deckhouse on either side of the No. 1 funnel. The latter could be raised up off the roof and lowered to the deck below by means of block and tackles that could be rigged to eyes spliced into the funnel shrouds above them.

The total lifeboat capacity was for 1,178 persons, well in excess of the official requirements – but more than 2,000 short of the number *Titanic* was certified to carry. Provision of sufficient life-boats became one of the most contentious issues that arose in the wake of the *Titanic* disaster. Much of the blame was levelled at the outdated regulations set by the British Board of Trade, which had not been amended since 1894.

At the time of the last revision of the Board of Trade life-boat regulations, the 12,950-ton Cunard vessel *Campania* was

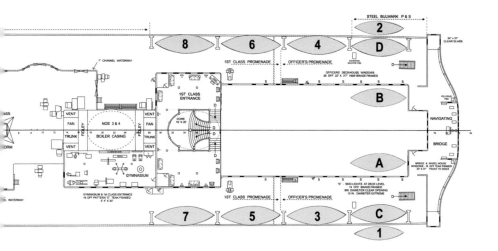

the largest ship afloat. In the years following this revision, no allowance was made for the dramatic increase in the size and passenger capacity of subsequent ships. At the time the plans were drawn for the construction of the *Olympic*-class ships in 1908, the regulations showed no distinction between the 12,950-ton *Campania* and the more than 46,000-ton *Olympic* and *Titanic*. Under the regulations in force at that time, all British vessels of more than 10,000 tons with sufficient watertight subdivisions only had to carry sixteen lifeboats with a total capacity of 990 persons.

Titanic was fitted with Marconi wireless communication. This feature was primarily installed aboard as a passenger amenity and not a navigational aid, however important messages addressed to the Captain were to have precedence. Passengers requesting messages to be sent by Marconi wireless were required to pay a sum for the communication through the ship's Purser's Office.

Navigational communication was received and dispatched as a courtesy offered by the Marconi Company to the ship owners. Because wireless was so new to passenger ships, the deck officers relied on the old standards of ship-to-ship communication as their experience at sea dictated.

Titanic's Marconi equipment was the most powerful possessed by any vessel of the mercantile marine. The 5kW wireless

Olympic's Marconi Wireless Operation Room, showing the instruments and equipment required to send and receive messages. *Titanic*'s Marconi wireless installation was identical, although the room was in a different location on the two ships. (Taken by Francis Browne/ author's collection)

transmitter was connected to four parallel aerial wires suspended between the ship's towering masts. From these aerial wires, cables led directly to the equipment in the wireless room.

The wireless installation consisted of two complete sets of apparatus: one for transmitting and the other for receiving transmissions, plus an emergency transmitting set with limited range that could operate independently of the ship's power supply for six hours. The main transmitter had a guaranteed minimum range of 400 miles. However, at night or during certain atmospheric conditions, its range extended to more than 2,000 miles.

The aerial array was supported by the two masts, 200ft high, stepped 600ft apart and had a mean height of 170ft. It was of the twin T-type and was used for the double purpose of transmitting and receiving. The wireless apparatus was manned twenty-four hours a day by two operators who were employed by the Marconi International Marine Communication Company Ltd.

10

First Class Grand Staircase Bronze Cherub and Pedestal

Among the most luxurious public spaces through-out *Titanic*'s First Class accommodations was the English oak staircase located inside the First Class Entrance Hall. It is perhaps the most recognised area of the ship's interior. Known by many as 'The Grand Staircase', an unofficial title, it is commonly represented by the carved rectangular oak pedestal supporting a bronze cherub which was located at the staircase landing on A Deck.

This bronze cherub is a historically accurate repro-duction of the one on *Olympic*. Alan St George, founder of titanicclock.com, utilised archival images from *Olympic* and the near identical forerunner that inspired the Harland & Wolff artisans as references. The original cherub is larger, being Pierre Granier's 'L'enfant avec la Torche' on Le Parterre d'Eau at Versailles.

The 36in-tall wooden pedestal is accurate to the original on *Olympic*. Alan recreated the piece in oak, with the exception of the intricately carved panels, which were cast in resin from an original *Olympic* pedestal carving in the collection of *Titanic* historian Ken Marshall. The carved panels each have unique arrangements of fruits, flowers and vegetables on all sides, just like the pedestals and newel posts on *Titanic* and *Olympic*. There were over 200 unique newel post panels integrated into the staircase and entrance foyers on each of the two ships.

When Thomas Ismay first employed decorative artists for his ships, furniture was of the horsehair-covered bench type. The ships' carpenters did their best as far as dining chairs and tables were concerned and the ships' painters undertook crude mural decorations. By the time of *Titanic*'s launch, the ocean liners far outstripped the hotels to which they were sometimes compared in their comfort, luxury and service. Though Third Class accommodations remained spartan in their simplicity, Second Class had gone far beyond any of the best accommodations available several decades earlier, and First Class accommodations were lavish in their appointments.

Harland & Wolff employed joiners and artisans to undertake the work of carving, plastering and fitting interior woodwork; the crafting either being carried out inside their own sheds within the shipyard or brought in from outside contractors. A large amount of the passenger and crew accommodation fittings were, of course, common stock, such as the many double and triple-hinged hooks seen about the rooms. These types of catalogue fittings were provided by firms such as George Field & Co. of Birmingham, which supplied many of the miscellaneous pieces on *Titanic*.

More specialised fittings would be fabricated as required; where this was done, fittings of every type – including furniture, panelling, mouldings, doors, relief carvings and brass castings – were drawn out on paper first. Later, specialist firms would supply pieces made from these drawings.

Opposite: The bronze cherub at the foot of *Olympic*'s forward First Class staircase at A Deck. There are no known images of *Titanic*'s First Class Grand Staircase, but it is known that both ships' interiors were nearly identical. (Author's collection)

11

First Class Staircase Cornice Moulding Section

A close up of the hand-carving from a small section of *Olympic*'s English oak First Class staircase cornice moulding, in the style of William and Mary.

British ocean liners of the Edwardian era traditionally followed a general overall design scheme, combining the features and comfort of a modern hotel with the luxury and opulence generally associated with a palace. The various public rooms and many of the most expensive staterooms were decorated in almost as many styles and combinations of styles as there were rooms to be adorned.

Every monarch's reign and every period of history of every nation after which a style was named had found use by the designers of the interiors and their furnishings. It was said that one could sleep in a bed whose design fitted the period of one monarch's rule; breakfast within the décor of another dynasty altogether; lunch under a different flag and furniture scheme; play cards, smoke or indulge in music under three other monarchs; have your afternoon cup of tea on a veranda that was more modern and cosmopolitan; and return in evening dress to experience dinner in one of the historical periods experienced earlier in the day.

In *Titanic*'s palatial First Class suites, one could see the Adam-style panelling, the oak of Louis XVI, the grey of Louis XV, the white of the Empire and the fine woodwork of the Italian Renaissance, not to mention Queen Anne, Regency, Modern Dutch and Old Dutch rooms. Such motifs were also employed skilfully and elegantly throughout the First and Second Class public rooms of the ship: the oak of the First Class Grand Staircase in the William and Mary style, the First Class Dining Saloon in Jacobean, the First Class Smoking Room and the First Class Reading and Writing Room in early and late Georgian respectively, and the Second Class Library in colonial Adam style, to name a few.

Titanic's interiors were designed in London, Liverpool and Belfast by Aldam Heaton & Co., this firm having worked on earlier White Star liners and the homes of the Ismay family. With the rush on in Belfast to complete *Olympic* in 1911, Aldam Heaton & Co. was taken over by International Mercantile Marine's Oceanic Transport Company, which was, for all intents and purposes, Harland & Wolff. The result was that the Belfast shipbuilders effectively had their own in-house decorators.

From the large dining saloons, lounges and restaurants, to the Second Class Library and the mahogany berths of the Third Class cabins; from Stuart crystal and china to glassware and unplated flatware, *Titanic* was a microcosm of Edwardian culture gathered together for seven days at sea.

12

Louis XV Dressing Table

This Louis XV-style, carved walnut knee-hole dressing table on cabriole legs is from one of the special period suites designed by Aldam Heaton & Co. It is originally from *Olympic*'s First Class stateroom C77, which was decorated in the Louis XV style. This is the same style as *Titanic*'s First Class stateroom C79, which is not known to have been occupied. C79 was one of two rooms that were connected with a 15-ton section of the *Titanic*'s shell plating that was raised from the wreck in August 1998 called 'The Big Piece'.

Brochures, magazines and newspapers all boasted of the eleven luxurious styles in which *Titanic*'s various bedrooms and sitting rooms were decorated. While this is an impressive array of popular styles from centuries past, the number is made even more impressive by designs created with variations of many of these styles. Consequently, there were nineteen unique representations of eleven period styles.

Additionally, there were two special styles of Harland & Wolff's own design. One, Harland & Wolff's 'Bedroom A' design, was reminiscent of Louis XV, with plainly but elegantly carved oak panels and elegant oak furniture on cabriole legs. This was referred to informally by Harland & Wolff as the French Cabin in Oak. The other, Harland & Wolff's 'Bedroom B' design, was not as luxurious as the period suites or the 'Bedroom A' design. This style had white panels with an oak dado and furniture consisting of the more familiar and common furnishings found in other First Class staterooms.

B Deck and C Deck were the only areas where the 'special staterooms' were located. Of the nineteen variations on *Titanic*, four styles were used in the four sitting rooms, with the remaining fifteen period style variations used for bedrooms, each of these styles being used twice. Thus, on *Titanic* (and *Olympic*) there were only thirty-four special staterooms decorated in a period style: fourteen on B Deck and twenty on C Deck (including two sitting rooms per deck).

13

Georgian Stateroom Door and Casing

A Georgian period-style stateroom door and casing from *Olympic*. **Items such as these only survive, thankfully, because they were bought at the Knight, Frank & Rutley auction of her fittings in 1935 and then reinstalled in private residences, offices, hotels and other locations scattered about the United Kingdom.**

Of the various period styles, the Regency style was used only once, in the sitting room of a parlour suite. It was panelled in rich mahogany accented with gilt details and carvings.

The Adam style, with its white panelling, had two variations: one was used for a sitting room and the other for a bedroom.

Louis XVI was used in a sitting room and two variations of bedrooms. The Louis XVI-style sitting room was decorated in carved walnut and sycamore panelling.

One of the bedroom variations was possibly similar in appearance but panelled in oak. This is the only variation for which there are no known photographs or illustrations to give any visual references. The other Louis XVI-style bedroom was designed and fitted out by H.P. Mutters & Zoon of Holland.

The style of Louis XIV, with its carved oak panels, was used in a sitting room and a bedroom. The Louis XV style was represented by only one design variation and was used in bedrooms.

The Georgian style had two variations and was also used in bedrooms. The early Georgian had carved walnut panelling and furniture, while the late Georgian used white panelling, accented by mouldings of fruit and flowers, with the furniture remaining carved walnut but differing slightly from that of the early Georgian style.

The Empire style had an impressive three variations of bedrooms. The third of which was designed and fitted out by H.P. Mutters & Zoon. The two bedroom variations in Modern Dutch were essentially the same in design. However, one was panelled in oak and furnished with brass bedsteads, while the other was panelled in sycamore and furnished with sycamore bedsteads; these, too, were also designed and fitted out by Mutters & Zoon. Designed by the same company, Old Dutch was also used in bedrooms with canopied beds.

An artist's impression of the early Georgian-style stateroom on *Olympic*. The one shown here – C80 – was the equivalent to C81 and C86 on *Titanic*. (*The Shipbuilder*/ author's collection)

Italian Renaissance had only one representation and was used in bedrooms. Queen Anne was likewise used once as a bedroom style.

The two special Harland & Wolff designs were used in the remaining large bedrooms on B and C Decks. Harland & Wolff's 'Bedroom A' design was used fourteen times and the 'Bedroom B' design was used twenty-nine times, with an additional two staterooms on A Deck also fitted in this style.

Titanic's interiors were installed from June 1911 up until the time she departed for her sea trials. (Final touch-ups and furniture arrangement was even done while at Southampton, where finishing touches were undertaken.) Over the next year, while moored alongside Harland & Wolff's outfitting wharf, shipfitters and interior decorators worked rigorously to install the famous carved woodwork, tiles and floor coverings. The amalgamation of all of these items became the famous interior, accommodations, public rooms, staterooms and cabins associated with *Titanic*.

14

First Class Bedstead

Titanic was furnished with very comfortable beds, some arranged as berths, one above the other, and some with bedsteads, as would be seen on land. A good number of the beds were fitted with hair mattresses on spring frames, intended to adjust themselves to the motion of the ship so that whenever the ship rolled or pitched, the bed remained somewhat horizontal.

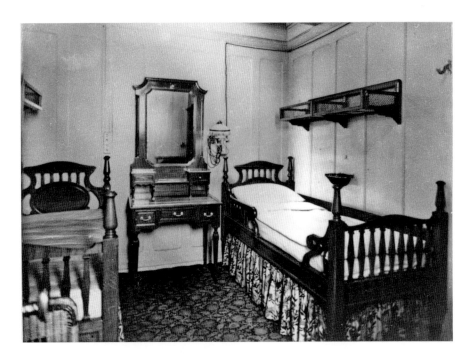

One of *Olympic*'s First Class cabins with bedsteads in view. The image effectively illustrates *Titanic*'s stateroom C113, and also gives an impression of staterooms C111, C118 and C120, as well as B99 to B102 on the deck above. (Author's collection)

Ships' berths, as far as possible, were arranged in a fore and aft direction, with the head of the bed usually pointing to the bow. There was greater rolling and more movement of the ship in an athwartship direction, hence the narrower part of the berth was oriented in this direction.

The cot bed, or bedstead, as is pictured on the previous page, was fitted in a First Class stateroom on *Britannic*. In many respects, it was similar to an ordinary household bed, supported on four legs that were framed to form two ends. The whole of the bed was enclosed by raised sides or leeboards, which served the purpose of preventing any movement of the mattress and bed linen when the ship was rolling. The spring and mattress, which were supported on laths screwed to the ends and side rails, varied in size to fit the bed frame.

All of the beds throughout the ship were secured to the deck with special fittings. When the bedsteads were made of wood, they generally matched the wood of the accompanying furniture in the room. Curtains, or 'valances', were fitted to the bottom of all First Class bedsteads to conceal the space beneath. In addition to being decorative, they were also functional. Passengers commonly stored trunks or bags under their bedsteads that would then be neatly concealed by the valances. When this was not the case, the valance would conceal ducting or piping that may have been run there.

All of the single berths in First Class consisted of cot beds made of brass, mahogany, oak, walnut and other woods. The brass cot beds on *Titanic* were supplied by Hoskins & Sewell Ltd, of Birmingham. Hoskins & Sewell also fitted their 'Tapex' spring mattresses to all berths throughout the First and Second Class accommodations, and their 'Orex' spring-and-chain mattresses to all berths in the Third Class cabins. They also supplied the galvanised metal bunks for the dormitory-type crew quarters, as well as the accommodations of the same type for the male steerage passengers.

Lights out was generally at 11.00 p.m., when the Dining Saloons closed. In First Class, the Lounge and the Reading and Writing Room remained open until 11.30 p.m. and the Smoke Room until midnight. In Second Class, the Library and the Smoke Room also closed at 11.30 p.m. In Third Class, female passengers were ordered off the decks at 9 or 10 o'clock by the Master-at-Arms, and men and women were requested to turn in at 10.30 p.m.

15

Turkish Bath Cooling Room Tiles

Persian-inspired Turkish Bath tiles made by Pilkington's Lancastrian Pottery & Tiles, presumably as samples for *Titanic* and *Olympic*. A panel and two spare tiles were loaned to a local gallery and when the company went into receivership in 2010, the tiles were sold by the administrators. This pattern was found in *Titanic*'s Cooling Room on the wreck, but in slightly different colours. They are shown here to represent the recreational facilities available for First Class passengers aboard *Titanic*.

Titanic's Turkish Bath was located on F Deck and included such amenities as Steam, Shampooing and Cooling Rooms as well as the Electric Bath. This facility did not involve bathing by immersing

oneself in a large body of water, as in a swimming bath. Rather, it involved sitting or lying down in a series of rooms of increasingly hot, dry air until the bather sweated profusely, followed by a cold shower or a plunge in a pool, then being given a full body wash and massage (called 'shampooing' by the Victorians) and finally relaxing in a cooling room until the body regained its normal temperature. This type of bath was not a true Turkish Bath, but rather a Victorian version of it, which was somewhat different in its characteristics and, in fact, drew inspiration from the Roman baths of antiquity.

Titanic's Cooling Room within the Turkish Bath facility on F Deck. (Author's collection)

Some bathers liked to weigh themselves before and after a Turkish Bath to see how much weight they had lost. Any weight loss would be purely temporary. For the average passenger, though, this was a harmless delusion, and an elaborate weighing chair was provided to give a feeling of satisfaction that some good had been achieved.

On *Titanic*, the Cooling Room was in many respects one of the most striking rooms on the ship. With its ornate tilework and exotic, seventeenth-century Arabesque décor, this is the room most often illustrated when *Titanic*'s Turkish Baths are described. The walls, from the dado to the cornice, were completely tiled in large panels of pale blue and green, surrounded by a broad band of tiles in a slightly bolder and deeper hue. The ceiling cornice and beams were gilt, with the intervening panels picked out in dull red with gilt detailing, from which were suspended electric lantern-style lamps of pierced and ornamental brass work. The dado, doors and panelling were teak. The stanchions, also cased in teak, were carved all over with an intricate Moorish pattern and surmounted by a carved cap.

An Electric Bath was located in a separate room off the fore and aft corridor between the Cooling Room and Shampooing Rooms. The Electric Bath provided a unique experience, which essentially involved the 'bather' lying down inside a large, insulated box that enclosed them from the neck down. A number of electric lamps fitted to the upper part of the unit radiated heat, thereby providing the bather much the same 'benefit' as experienced by those using the Hot Room of the Turkish Baths. In many ways, the unit resembled one of the 'iron lungs' seen in hospitals of the 1950s. The Electric Bath was only available by appointment and required supervision by an attendant the entire time it was in use.

16

Swimming Bath Tile

These tiles, manufactured by Villeroy & Boch, were used extensively on *Olympic* and *Titanic*, but most notably in the area of the Swimming Bath. This First Class feature was on F Deck, conveniently located next to the Turkish Baths.

The Swimming Bath was a unique luxury and not yet common aboard ships at the time. Utilising saltwater, it was filled from the ship's mains via the hot saltwater tank on the Boat Deck in conjunction with cold saltwater let into the inlet of the pool from a separate pipe. Filling was not begun, however, until the vessel was at sea, as the cold water used with the bath was initially pumped in from the condenser intakes, and the quality of the water near port was not very clean.

The Swimming
Bath aboard
Titanic.
(Author's
collection)

The Swimming Bath was 33ft x 14ft with an average depth of 5ft. To port of the Swimming Bath, along the inboard bulkhead, was a row of thirteen dressing cubicles with partitioning and doors of mahogany. The compartment within which the Swimming Bath was located also included two combined needle-spray shower baths fitted with nickel-plated taps and piped with fresh water. Despite the otherwise plain décor and fittings of the overall space, the showers were set within decorative enclosures and were finished floor to ceiling in artistically decorative ceramic tiles.

The Swimming Bath was well patronised by the passengers. For those having purchased a ticket to the Turkish Baths, there was no additional charge to use it. Passengers could use the Swimming Bath for free without a Turkish Bath ticket, but only in the morning between 6.00 and 9.00 a.m. Outside of the free-use hours there was a fee, for which tickets were available from the Enquiry Office at a charge of 25 cents each. Though White Star Line brochures do not indicate the hours during which ladies could make use of the bath free of charge, records from *Olympic*'s first three voyages do show that this practice was carried out.

The luxurious accommodations for the First Class passengers were augmented by the addition of a well-equipped gymnasium situated on the Boat Deck, immediately abaft the forward main staircase and a squash court on G Deck.

PART III

TITANIC GOES TO SEA

Titanic during
her sea trials
on 2 April
1912. (Author's
collection)

As was general practice for new liners preparing to enter commercial service, the captain and senior officers would arrive early at the shipbuilder's yard to acquaint themselves with their new charge. Captain Edward Smith and his seven deck officers came to Belfast during the month of March 1912 to be with the ship during her final stages of fitting out.

Captain Smith had commanded *Olympic* since she had entered commercial service, the year before, and with him came William Murdoch, also from *Olympic*, as Chief Officer; First Officer Charles H. Lightoller from *Oceanic*; Second Officer David Blair from *Teutonic*; Third Officer Herbert Pitman; Fourth Officer Joseph Boxhall and Fifth Officer Harold Lowe. Included with the other senior crew members joining at Belfast were the engineering officers, headed by Chief Joseph Bell, and the two Marconi wireless operators, John 'Jack' Phillips and Harold Bride.

Titanic's sea trials had been planned for Monday, 1 April 1912. The required tugs, owned by the Alexander Towing Company, had been dispatched from Liverpool to Belfast on 31 March. The weather was bitter and cold with a strong north-westerly wind, turning the normally calm Victoria Channel rough and choppy. By 10.00 a.m., the scheduled time of *Titanic's* departure, it was decided that the conditions in the channel presented too great a risk for safe ship handling and the trials were postponed until the following day.

By the next morning, conditions had improved considerably and a clear sky and calm waters no doubt caused more than one officer and tug captain to breathe more easily. The tugs *Herculaneum*, *Hornby*, *Hercules*, *Herald* and *Huskisson* escorted *Titanic* up the channel with Captain Smith in command, Smith having handed over command of *Olympic* to Captain Herbert James Haddock a short time earlier.

Once in the open waters of Belfast Lough, *Titanic* was put through a series of manoeuvres to test her turning and stopping capabilities and other aspects of her performance. Although her sea trials were not as rigorous as those *Olympic* had undergone the year before, they were by no means perfunctory. As both ships had identical hulls and propulsion machinery, there was no need to determine what *Titanic*'s handling characteristics were, only to verify that she performed as expected and required.

While *Titanic* was being put through her paces, Phillips and Bride were tuning and testing the ship's Marconi system and relaying messages back and forth from owner to shipbuilder.

Titanic returned to Belfast at 6.30 p.m. that evening and was obliged to lower both starboard and port anchors under the critical eye of the Board of Trade surveyor, Francis Carruthers. Being satisfied with the ship's performance throughout the trials, Carruthers signed the certificate of seaworthiness, which was valid for one year. With this document in hand, the directors of the White Star Line would have seen the obligations of the contract finalised, thereby acknowledging the official transfer of the vessel from builder to owner.

With the formalities dispensed with and the transfer of the officials ashore, *Titanic* weighed anchor around 8.00 p.m. Departing Belfast Lough, she briefly tracked eastward into the Irish Sea and made for Southampton. During the 570-mile trip, the officers took the opportunity to perform additional engine and manoeuvring tests.

17
Royal Naval Reserve Sword and Belt

As the new, big ship in the fleet, *Titanic* had the pick of the White Star crews, and for her maiden voyage she would be commanded by the line's senior Captain, 62-year-old Commander Edward John Smith RD (Retired) RNR (Royal Naval Reserve). Smith's RNR sword was identical to the example pictured here.

Smith joined the Royal Naval Reserve in 1888 and served as a Transport Captain during the Boer War. Later, he would receive the Transport Medal and also the officer's decoration and rank of commander in recognition for his long and dedicated service with the RNR.

If a ship was commanded by an officer of the Royal Naval Reserve and had at least ten RNR officers and/or crew aboard, an Admiralty warrant could be issued to permit the flying of the Blue Ensign. Captain Smith held such a warrant – No. 690 – and this had to be noted on the ship's Articles of Agreement. (It should also be noted that members of the Royal Naval Reserve were not necessarily former naval personnel – they could also be merchant marine personnel who joined the Naval Reserve and received a limited amount of training.) With this fact, *Titanic* was able to fly the Blue Ensign from her stern pole.

Known affectionately as 'E.J.', Smith was born in Hanley, Staffordshire, in 1850. His career at sea began as an apprentice in 1867 at the age of 17, with the Liverpool shippers Andrew Gibson & Co.

Smith gained his Ordinary Master's certificate (No. 14102) in 1875. He joined the White Star Line in 1880, serving as Fourth Officer on their 3,867-ton *Celtic*. He commanded the White Star Line's *Republic* (I) for a brief time in 1887. The following year he achieved his Extra Master's Certificate and eventually took charge of the *Baltic* (I). During his service with White Star, Smith would command a total of fourteen vessels.

E.J. Smith had a good reputation as an ocean liner Captain, with a following among frequent travellers. People would book passage on the White Star ships that Smith commanded because they liked him. He was a good-natured man and looked the traditional role of an old sea salt with his beer barrel-shaped body and his grey beard and kind eyes.

He was noted as a stickler for ship's discipline but was well liked by his crew, a highly skilled seaman but a bit of a showman. In 1907, Captain Smith made a foreboding statement to a *New York Times* reporter:

When anyone asks me how I can best describe my experience in nearly 40 years at sea, I merely say – uneventful. Of course there have been winter storms and gales and fog and the like, but in all my experience I have never been in an accident of any sort worth speaking about. I have seen but one vessel in distress in all my years at sea – a brig, the crew of which was taken off in a small boat in charge of my third officer. I never saw a wreck and have never wrecked, nor was I ever in any predicament that threatened to end in disaster of any sort. You see, I am not very good material for a story.

There had been a number of slight incidents involving the ships he had captained in the past, but these happenings were while the ships were under the command of harbour pilots. By 1912, Smith had been at sea for forty-five years, thirty-two of those with White Star. He was the most highly paid sea-farer in the world, earning £1,250 a year, and because of the clientele he now attracted, he was widely regarded as the 'millionaires' captain'.

It was surely because of Smith's popularity that White Star gave him command of their new super liners as they entered service, the *Olympic* in 1911 and her sister, *Titanic* in 1912. It was stated that Captain Smith was to retire after the maiden voyage of *Titanic*, but this has not been substantiated.

Captain Edward John Smith. (Author's collection)

Southampton, Cherbourg and Queenstown

At approximately 10.00 p.m. on the evening of 3 April, *Titanic* steamed past the Isle of Wight, then slowed at the Nab Lightship for the embarkation of the Southampton pilot. With the pilot now on her bridge, *Titanic* proceeded cautiously at half-ahead past Cowes, rounded the Brambles Sandbank and into Southampton Water. A short period later, five Red Star tugs – *Ajax, Hector, Hercules, Neptune* and *Vulcan* – assisted the ship into the calm waters of the River Test. The time was just after 11.30 p.m.

It was just after midnight when *Titanic* was finally secured along-side Berth 44. On the morning of Thursday, 4 April, Southampton awoke to find *Titanic* dressed in flags, a custom in the maritime community to signify the first day in a new ship's port city. The city residents would have special reason to show pride in *Titanic*, as Southampton would be her home port of departure even though she was registered in Liverpool.

Due to delays during the fitting out in Belfast, *Titanic* had to forgo the customary stop at Liverpool while en route to Southampton, as her sister had done the year prior. Harland & Wolff had to under-take some finishing touches to White Star's newest ship quickly, as the sailing date of her maiden voyage was less than a week away. Last-minute painting and decorating was undertaken as well as the fitting of some interior fixtures, while the ship was being pro-visioned. To complicate the time restraints, Good Friday and Easter Sunday would cause the loss of two days of work. Because of this, *Titanic* was not opened for public inspection but only for a small number of press photographers and reporters who were allowed onto the upper decks and promenades.

Titanic's officers and senior crew were aboard in Southampton, standing regular watches and overseeing the loading of supplies, stowage of cargo and the final preparatory duties for sailing. Those crew members consisted generally of the Engine Room men as stewards and seamen were not due aboard until sailing day. The official signing on list bore the notation, 'Date and hour at which he is to be on board: 6 a.m. 10.4.12.'

Titanic dressed in flags as a salute to her home port on Thursday, 4 April 1912. (Author's collection)

Titanic was certified for 905 First Class passengers, 564 Second Class, 1,134 Third Class and a crew of 944, making a total capacity of 3,547. On this voyage, *Titanic* would carry 2,208 people in all.

The crew numbered 891, 500 of whom, such as cooks, stewards, store and laundry attendants, looked directly after the passengers. There were 325 crewmen actively employed in the mechanical workings of the ship, such as firemen, trimmers, engineers and electricians. In addition, there were sixty-six crewmen who belonged to the Deck Department. They comprised lookouts, quartermasters and able seamen, including the two wireless operators. *Titanic* laid silent in her berth on Good Friday, 5 April, with a minimum number of crewmen keeping watch.

18

Assistant Butcher Christopher Mills' Discharge Book and Pocket Watch

Saturday, 6 April was the hiring date for the remaining crew needed for the maiden voyage. Among the crew to sign on was Assistant Butcher Christopher Mills who, according to his discharge book, gave an address of 94 Albert Road, Southampton. Mills survived the sinking, and these items, consisting of his discharge book and pocket watch, came off the ship with him.

Most of the stokers and trimmers, known as the 'Black Gang', were taken from Southampton, and the unions had no problem supplying workers to meet *Titanic*'s complement. A coal miners' strike had been on throughout Great Britain since 12 January 1912, causing many ships to be laid up due to a lack of fuel. The coal loaded aboard *Titanic* in Southampton was taken from other White Star Line ships that lay idle, with extra coal brought in advance by *Olympic* from New York.

Work aboard *Titanic* halted once again on Easter Sunday, 7 April. But on Monday, 8 April, the dock was a flurry of movement. Given the vast quantities of stores that were needed on every voyage, orders would need to be placed well in advance, and would begin arriving at the dockside far ahead of the next sailing date.

This assemblage of stores was considerable. Foods were ordered from many parts of the globe: choice fruits from California, cheese from all over Europe, oysters from Baltimore, ice cream from New York, coffee from Brazil, tea from India, mutton from the Berkshire Downs, and so on. The White Star Line also contracted store merchants such as Grey & Co. to provide other food supplies.

The average consumption of stores for *Olympic*, enumerated in the following particulars, were supplied by the White Star Line and may be considered as a fair average of what the company had to provide every time she left Southampton:

> *Fresh meats, 75,000lb; fresh fish, 11,000lb; salt and dried fish, 4,000lb; bacon and ham, 7,500lb; poultry and game, 8,000 head; fresh butter, 6,000lb; fresh eggs, 40,000; sausages, 2,500lb; sweetbreads, 1,000; ice cream, 1,750 quarts; coffee, 2,200lb; tea, 800lb; peas, rice etc., 10,000lb; sugar, 10,000lb; jams, 1,120lb; flour, 200 barrels; potatoes, 40 tons; apples, 180 boxes; oranges, 180 boxes (36,000); lemons, 50 boxes (16,000); hothouse grapes, 1,000; fresh milk, 1,500gal.; condensed milk, 600gal.; grape fruit, 50 boxes; lettuces, 7,000; cream, 1,000 quarts; fresh asparagus, 800 bundles; onions, 3,500lb; fresh green peas, 1¼ tons; tomatoes, 2¾ tons; beer and stout, 20,000 bottles; mineral waters, 15,000 bottles; wines, 1,500 bottles; spirits, 850 bottles; cigars, 8,000.*

19

White Star Line Binoculars

Pictured here are a pair of White Star Line-issued binoculars and case. The binoculars were made in Belfast by Sharman Neill, a Belfast optician, who manufactured a number of other instruments for *Titanic* and other White Star ships.

Captain Smith's deck officers, who had been with *Titanic* since Belfast, underwent a late-hour reshuffle on 9 April. Henry T. Wilde was brought on board as Chief Officer, as he had served with Captain Smith in that position on *Olympic*. This position was originally assigned to William Murdoch, who was bumped down to first officer. As a consequence, Second Officer David

Blair was removed altogether. Charles Lightoller, originally first officer, now stepped back to second. The junior officers remained the same, with Herbert Pitman, Joseph Boxhall, Harold Lowe and James Moody.

An apocryphal tale, which unfortunately has been carved into *Titanic*'s history, is about Second Officer David Blair's binoculars. The story is that a pair of binoculars designated for the lookouts' use had been stored in a locker within Blair's quarters. It is believed that the change of deck officers at Southampton took place suddenly, and in the process, Blair was sent ashore, to be replaced by Lightoller, still with his keys in his pocket.

In August 2007, some of Blair's personal items from *Titanic* (and other ships he served on) were brought to auction. One of the items was a key with an attached fob stamped 'Binocular Box'. The news media translated this information to read that there was only one pair of binoculars on *Titanic*, and that Blair had the only key to access the binocular box. Somehow, the ship's binocular box made it into Blair's cabin, and with no binoculars, the lookouts could not see the iceberg fast enough.

All White Star ships (generally, all commercial ships) had a box located on the bridge containing owner-supplied binoculars for the deck officers. Therefore, all of the deck officers would have been issued a 'binocular box' key. It was revealed in testimony, after the sinking, that Second Officer David Blair had allowed the two lookouts in the crow's nest to use his binoculars from Belfast to Southampton. After arriving in Southampton, Blair ordered lookout George Hogg to lock the binoculars in his quarters (the locker in his quarters) and return the key to him. Hogg stated the binoculars were inscribed 'Second Officer, S.S. *Titanic*'.

As has been stated earlier, Blair was sent ashore after being replaced by Lightoller as second officer. In disembarking the ship, Blair took his company-issued keys with him, which included the key for the locker in the Second Officer's Quarters, as well as other ship's keys. Suddenly, the lack of binoculars for the lookouts on the night of 14 April became fodder for the news media in 2007 and onward.

The fact that the lookouts had no binoculars aboard *Titanic* was not unusual for the time. Captains of other ships and *Titanic*'s surviving officers all verified that binoculars were not generally issued to lookouts. They cited many reasons for this, but ultimately it was the decision of the captain or the officer of the watch. A pair of binoculars was issued by the shipping company to each senior officer and, when the officer was on duty, could be temporarily stowed in a teak box located on the bulwark of either bridge wing. The company binoculars were stowed in a felt-lined teak box located in the Chart Room when not in use. An additional pair of binoculars was provided for the Harbour Pilot and were commonly referred to as 'Pilot Glasses'.

20

White Star Line Officer's Hat

After the reshuffling of *Titanic*'s deck officers, the final line-up of men was impressive, in relation to their experience at sea. Most of them had already earned their Master's certificates, and all were members of the Royal Naval Reserve, except Third Officer Pitman. This period White Star Line officer's hat is the same type as those that were worn by *Titanic*'s senior officers during the winter season, which included mid-April 1912.

Henry Tingle Wilde RNR, Chief Officer

Second in command was Henry Tingle Wilde RNR, the 38-year-old Chief Officer of *Titanic* who was responsible for the safe-keeping of the ship's logbook. Wilde earned his Extra Master's Certificate in 1900, having joined White Star in 1897 as fourth officer on *Cevic*, and rapidly climbed the ranks. At the time of the *Titanic* disaster, Wilde held a lieutenant's commission in the Royal Naval Reserve, having joined the RNR in 1902.

In August 1911, Wilde was appointed as Chief Officer of *Olympic* for her second voyage to New York. Then, during the sinking of *Titanic*, he supervised the readying and lowering of the lifeboats and distributed hand-guns among senior officers to maintain order on the deck.

Chief Officer Henry Wilde. (Author's collection)

William McMaster Murdoch RNR, First Officer

William McMaster Murdoch was the 39-year-old first officer on *Titanic*. Murdoch completed his apprenticeship in 1892, attaining an Extra Master's certificate in 1896, prior to joining White Star in 1899. He too served as a Royal Navy Reservist, and in 1903, his 'derring-do', snatching the wheel of *Arabic* himself, saved the ship from collision with another vessel.

Posted as first officer of *Titanic*, Murdoch would achieve noto-riety for being in command of the bridge the moment *Titanic*

First Officer
William
Murdoch.
(Author's
collection)

struck the iceberg. He assembled the passengers on the Boat Deck to have them board the lifeboats and was subsequently placed in charge of lowering those along its starboard side. Second Officer Charles Lightoller reported that he was last seen attempting to launch the collapsible lifeboats stored on the roof of the officers' quarters.

Charles Herbert Lightoller RNR, Second Officer

Second Officer
Charles
Lightoller.
(Author's
collection)

Charles Herbert Lightoller was Captain Smith's 38-year-old second officer. He was apprenticed to the sea in 1888. Following a varied early career, which included being shipwrecked in the Indian Ocean on a small uninhabited island for eight days in 1889 and a stint in the Yukon Gold Rush, he signed with White Star in January 1900 as fourth officer.

Attaining his Extra Master's certificate in 1902, Lightoller worked his way up the White Star Line's ships, from cattle transports like *Bovic* and *Georgic* to *Oceanic* and *Majestic*. He was trans-ferred from *Oceanic* to serve as first officer on *Titanic*, but he was demoted temporarily to make way for Wilde's impromptu appointment as chief.

After the collision, Lightoller was placed in charge of lowering the port-side lifeboats, famously obeying his Captain's order of 'women and children first' to the letter, even to the point of allow-ing seats to remain unfilled when neither women nor children were available to occupy them.

Wilde had ordered Lightoller to leave the ship in Collapsible Lifeboat D, but the second officer characteristically declined. Going down with *Titanic*, Lightoller managed to swim to an upturned Collapsible Lifeboat B, taking command of it and its thirty occupants standing upon its capsized hull until they were later rescued by other lifeboats.

As the most senior officer to survive *Titanic*, Lightoller endured the wrath of his inquisitor's probing during the American and British hearings.

Third Officer Herbert Pitman. (Author's collection)

Herbert John Pitman, Third Officer

Herbert John Pitman was the 34-year-old third officer of *Titanic*. He joined the sea in 1895, and subsequently White Star in 1906, immediately upon attaining his Ordinary Master's certificate. Not a member of the Royal Naval Reserve, he served previously aboard *Oceanic* as fourth officer before transferring to *Titanic*.

During the sinking, he helped lower her starboard lifeboats and was placed in charge of boat No. 5 by First Officer Murdoch.

Joseph Grove Boxhall RNR, Fourth Officer

Fourth Officer
Joseph Boxhall.
(Author's
collection)

Joseph Grove Boxhall, aged 28, was the fourth officer and principal navigator on *Titanic*. He joined the sea in 1899 as an apprentice with the William Thomas Line out of Liverpool. Gaining his Extra Master's certificate in 1907, he joined White Star that November. Prior to receiving his posting on *Titanic*, he served aboard *Oceanic* and *Arabic*.

A highly competent navigator, Boxhall was Captain Smith's preferred choice to chart the daily position of *Titanic* and earned notoriety for plotting her infamous CQD position. He was also first to inspect *Titanic* after the impact with the iceberg, albeit failing to find any damage.

Later that evening, Boxhall requested use of the distress rockets, which he and Quartermaster George Rowe then launched to summon help. The Captain ordered him command of Lifeboat 2, from which he continued firing flares to attract rescue ships, which were subsequently seen by *Carpathia*.

Harold Godfrey Lowe, RNR Fifth Officer

Aged 29, the fifth officer of *Titanic* was Harold Godfrey Lowe. He ran away to sea around 1898, working his way up 'through the hawsepipe' from ordinary seaman to deck officer. He gained his Ordinary Master's certificate in 1910 while serving with the Elder Dempster Line and joined the White Star Line in April 1911 as third officer of *Tropic*.

The maiden voyage of *Titanic* happened also to be his first Atlantic crossing. Following the collision, he worked under First

Officer Murdoch in lowering the forward starboard lifeboats and then joined Sixth Officer Moody to lower the aft port lifeboats.

Lowe took command of Lifeboat 14, and, after reaching the water, ordered Lifeboats 4, 10, 12 and Collapsible D to tie up to his own as *Titanic* sank. He then transferred his passengers into the other boats and assembled a crew to search for survivors, finding only four still alive, one of whom soon died. When dawn arrived, he raised a sail, took Collapsible D in tow, and on his way to the rescue ship *Carpathia*, rescued survivors who were standing on top of overturned Collapsible A.

Fifth Officer Harold Lowe. (Author's collection)

James Pell (Paul) Moody RNR, Sixth Officer

Twenty-four-year-old James Paul Moody was *Titanic's* sixth officer. He joined the training ship HMS *Conway* in Liverpool at the age of 14 and in 1904 joined the William Thomas Line as an apprentice.

After transferring to steam, much of his early career was spent on the South American run, on early oil tankers and tramp steamers. He gained his Ordinary Master's certificate in 1911 and then joined the White Star's *Oceanic* in August that year as sixth officer, promoted in January 1912 to fifth officer.

Sixth Officer James Moody. (Author's collection)

In March 1912, he requested leave from the line but was instructed instead to join *Titanic* as sixth officer. On the night of the sinking, he answered the lookout's telephoned alert, warning 'iceberg, right ahead', and recorded the time of the collision for the log. Afterwards, he circulated boat assignments to the crew and helped supervise the loading of the port-side boats.

Moody relinquished his lifeboat seat to his senior, Harold Lowe, and was last seen attempting to launch a collapsible boat stowed upon the roof of the bridge.

Joseph Bell, Chief Engineer

The Chief Engineer on *Titanic* was 51-year-old veteran Joseph Bell. Bell had joined the sea in 1883 and subsequently White Star in 1885. Promoted to Chief Engineer at the age of 30, he later served on *Olympic* prior to his posting to *Titanic*, which began even while it was undergoing construction.

During the sinking, Bell remained alongside his team of thirty-four engineers to maintain electricity to the ship's water pumps and lighting systems. Relieving his men of their duty at 2 a.m., all declined and remained at their posts to the bitter end. Bell perished, along with his entire engineering staff.

Chief Engineer Joseph Bell. (Author's collection)

The Marconi Telegraphists

Marconi Wireless Operators Jack Phillips (left) and Harold Bride. (Author's collection)

The two Marconi telegraphists were considered *Titanic* crew members, as they were paid by the White Star Line, but were actually employees of the Marconi Company. Having joined *Titanic* at Belfast, they elected to go ashore at Southampton.

Jack Phillips signed the ship's articles on 6 April, while Harold Bride signed on 9 April. The two men were busy during their time aboard in preparing their equipment for sailing day.

A constant wireless watch was maintained by the two men, working on a mutually agreed-upon rotation of Phillips from 8 a.m. to 2 p.m. and then 8 p.m. to 2 a.m., and Bride from 2 a.m. to 8 a.m. and 2 p.m. to 8 p.m.

21

Shipyard Toolkit of Guarantee Group Member Artie Frost

Anthony 'Artie' Wood Frost was employed by Harland & Wolff as a Foreman Fitter in the Engine Works. He and his wife, Lizzie Jane, had four children – one of whom, Marjorie, was the president of the Ulster *Titanic* Society until her death in 1995.

Artie started work at Harland & Wolff as a machine boy in 1888, at the age of 14. A year later, he was promoted to an apprentice fitter. After finishing his apprenticeship, he left Harland & Wolff and went to sea to gain experience for two years. Upon his return, he once again worked at Harland & Wolff, where he eventually came to be Leading Hand in 1901.

Artie's father, G.W. Frost, was a Foreman Fitter in the shipyard, and when he retired in 1907, Artie took over his job. Artie supervised the fitting of the machinery on board *Olympic* and *Titanic*.*

The Harland & Wolff Guarantee Group were hand picked and represented their respective departments pertaining to *Titanic*'s construction. The task of the men was to ensure that *Titanic* operated to the requirements guaranteed by the shipbuilder in its contractual obligations to the owner of the vessel. These men also took note of any modifications that might need to be undertaken in the future.

Under the supervision of Managing Director Thomas Andrews were William Parr, Assistant Manager of the Electrical Department; Roderick Chisholm, Chief Ship's Draughtsman; Anthony Frost, Outside Foreman Manager; Robert Knight, Leading Hand Fitter Engineer; William Campbell, Joiner Apprentice; Alfred Cunningham, Fitter Apprentice; Francis Parkes, Plumber Apprentice; and Ennis Watson, Electrical Apprentice. Andrews, Chisholm and Parr travelled in First Class while the others were berthed in Second Class.

Thomas (Tommy) Andrews was a personable man, and it was said of him that it was not sufficient to say that his colleagues liked him – they loved him. He had an innate courtesy and his chivalry made him unconscious of all class distinctions.** The crewmen on *Titanic* who knew him liked him very much, as he listened to and respected them.

---

*   Cameron, Stephen, *Titanic: Belfast's Own* (Dublin: Wolfhound Press, 1998).
** Cameron, Stephen, *Titanic: Belfast's Own* (Dublin: Wolfhound Press, 1998).

22

White Star Line Third Class Ticket Book

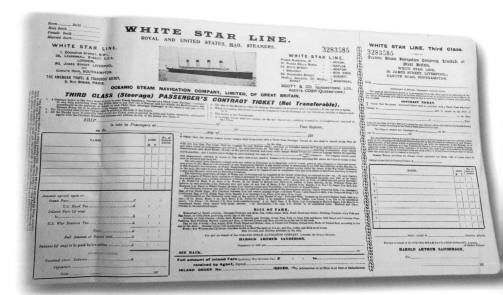

The tickets for each class of *Titanic*'s passengers represented a contract for passage between the company and the purchaser. Tickets for First Class were printed on tan paper; Second Class on buff and Third Class on white paper, as seen here. This example of a White Star Line ticket book from the 1920s is very similar to the 1912 version. The photographic image of *Olympic* and the removal of Joseph Bruce Ismay's name in exchange for Harold Arthur Sanderson are just two examples of the differences between this example and what was used in 1912.

In Southampton, 10 April 1912 dawned cool and cloudy. Soon after sunrise, *Titanic*'s crew started to emerge on the dock and carried on their duties throughout the morning. Captain Smith, having spent the night at his home in Southampton, arrived before 7 a.m. The other deck officers were already signed on, but those who went ashore had returned to the ship by midnight the night before.

Captain Maurice Clarke, the Board of Trade's Immigration Officer at Southampton, had inspected the ship. It was his task to certify that *Titanic* complied with the Merchant Shipping Acts as an emigrant ship. Having found all crew and passenger service appliances and equipment in good order, he directed the manning and lowering of two lifeboats under the supervision of Fifth Officer Lowe and Sixth Officer Moody.

The crew were required to muster on deck; each department in their predetermined locations. The muster list was called out and then the crewmen were checked and passed in front of a medical officer and Captain Clarke. Having verified the muster lists for the crew to be correct and in good order, he then signed the official paperwork that cleared *Titanic* fit to sail.

Ship's surgeons William O'Loughlin and J. Edward Simpson met with the Board of Trade medical representative to complete their paperwork on the crew's health. Meanwhile, Captain Clarke, with Captain Benjamin Steele, White Star's Marine Superintendent at Southampton, met with Captain Smith to hand over their reports.

Among the crewmen listed on Captain Smith's muster list were five sea post clerks, eight musicians, and sixty-nine employees servicing the new À La Carte Restaurant. The staff of the restaurant, which was run as a contracted concession, were employees of Luigi Gatti's London restaurants. Though not White Star employees, they signed the ship's articles and were paid one shilling for the voyage.

Sometime before the passengers arrived on the boat train, the Trinity House Harbour Pilot George Bowyer arrived and went up to the bridge to prepare for his duties at the time of sailing. 'Uncle George' Bowyer was an old timer and was well known to *Titanic*'s officers and other White Star crewmen using Southampton's port.

Bowyer was one of the pilots responsible for guiding ships in and out of the narrow, dredged waters of Southampton and would depart *Titanic* via a rowboat at the Nab Lightship, which was anchored at the point where the locally controlled pilotage waters opened to the sea.

J. Bruce Ismay and family boarded *Titanic* at about 9.30 a.m., having spent the night at the Southwestern Hotel, which is located just across from the White Star dock.* Ismay's personal secretary, William Henry Harrison, was also travelling to assist with the needs of his employer.

Passengers started arriving at the dock around 8.30 a.m. Many had stayed the night at nearby boarding houses and local hotels. While the passengers slept in anticipation of the next day's boarding, the dock had remained busy throughout the night, with stevedores handling provisions and putting them on board.

Of the two boat trains servicing the White Star dock, the first arrived at 9.30 a.m. from Waterloo station in London, carrying Second and Third Class passengers. The custom was to embark the Third Class and steerage passengers first, about two or three hours before the vessel sailed. This was not because they paid the lowest fares, but because there were so many of them. The number of children in this class was proportionately greater than in any other, and sufficient time had to be allowed for them to settle down before the voyage began.

It was not uncommon for the major steamship companies to provide temporary housing ashore for Third Class passengers who awaited transport on their ships. The White Star Line, being no exception, provided accommodations at their emigrant home in Southampton.

---

*   Ismay's family would leave the ship before *Titanic* sailed.

23
Third Class Steward's Jacket

Once the Third Class passengers boarded, they were directed to
their quarters rapidly and efficiently. The Third Class stewards,
who wore jackets similar to the one shown on the prior page, had
a well-organised routine, which functioned admirably to handle
hundreds of people who were completely unfamiliar with ships.
It would be common to hear a steward yell out, 'Single men this
way, please. Let me see your ticket – thank you. Straight along
the passage. You will find a steward a little further on who will
direct you.'

The next steward would probably have stationed himself at the
head of a staircase. 'Go down the stairs and turn left. Here, you sir,
you to the right. You all together? Yes, that way, to the right.' And
so it would continue, with passengers directed to their quarters,
where other stewards were in attendance to see that each man was
shown his berth with as little delay as possible.

The tickets were numbered to correspond to the sections of the
ship and the numbers of the berths. Thanks to this arrangement
and the careful directions of the stewards, the early arrivals
were, for the most part, soon on deck again watching other
passengers arrive.

Sympathetic stewardesses received the women and their children; families were directed to their multi-berth cabins; the
youngest single women, who were as often as not the daughters
of married couples aboard, were directed to quarters that were
specially reserved for them in the after end of the ship.

More than one child came aboard tired, crying and hungry.
The mother, perhaps in nearly the same condition herself if she
chose to admit it, probably rested on the first available seat and
endeavoured to compose herself and her family. She would soon
be taken in charge by a stewardess or matron. 'Come with me,
please. Here, this is your berth. You can sit here while your luggage is brought, and when Baby goes to sleep you can put him
in the berth. Hungry? Yes, dinner will be served as soon as the
steamer starts. It is not long to wait now, and in the meantime,
I'll see if I can get you a cup of tea and the children some biscuits.'

Many of the Third Class passengers embarking at Southampton
were Scandinavians. The White Star Line advertised extensively

throughout Norway and Sweden and had a large number of ticket agents in these areas.

Over the years since the *Titanic* tragedy, history has been generally twisted to suggest that there was some form of conscious segregation of the different nationalities in Third Class, but the fact of the matter is that the foreign sales agents were issued ticket books with specific blocks of rooms. It was the ticket books that caused groups of people to be segregated. The Scandinavians were berthed among other Scandinavians, and Middle Easterners with Middle Easterners, etc. because they purchased tickets from local agents who were issued books with pre-blocked rooms.

Over 240 Second Class passengers boarded at Southampton, finding their accommodations generally located on D, E and F Decks, which were as elegant as, or better than, First Class on some other liners. The Second Class passengers embarked about an hour (sometimes less) before the ship was due to depart.

Upon arriving, they were guided directly to their quarters by the stewards of their area. It was not unusual for a number of Second Class passengers and their visitors to stop by some of the First Class accommodations prior to sailing time. One such passenger was Mr Lawrence Beesley, a Dulwich College science master, who had the opportunity to ride the bicycle machine in the First Class gymnasium with his female friend who came to see him off.

Among the people boarding were *Titanic*'s eight musicians, who were booked as Second Class passengers under a contract with Messrs C.W. and F.N. Black, Musical Directors of Liverpool. *Titanic*'s musicians were, in fact, two separate units consisting of a quintet and a trio.

The quintet performed at specific places and times within the First and Second Class main companionways and did not perform during supper. The quintet was led by Bandmaster Wallace Hartley on violin, with John Wesley Woodward, cellist; John Law Hume, second violin; John Fredrick Preston Clarke on bass violin; and pianist Theodore Brailey.

The trio of musicians consisted of Georges Alexander Krins (leader) on violin, Percy Taylor on piano and Roger Bricoux on cello. The trio played specifically in the À La Carte Restaurant

1. MR. F. CLARKE, OF LIVERPOOL.   2. MR. P. C. TAYLOR, OF CLAPHAM.
...INS, OF BRIXTON, SOMETIME OF THE RITZ HOTEL ORCHESTRA.   4. MR. W. HARTLEY (BANDMASTER), OF DEWSBURY.   5. MR. W. T. BRAILEY, OF NOT...
6. MR. J. HUME, OF DUMFRIES.   7. MR. J. W. WOODWARD, OF HEADINGTON, OXON.

Reception Room on B Deck. The musicians had cabins on E Deck in Second Class but in a specific location where they were given an extra compartment adjacent to their quarters to secure their instruments.

First Class passengers arrived at 11.30 a.m., a mere half an hour before sailing time, and this was a more ceremonious affair than for the other classes. It was the custom of British liners to run a special train from London to the nearest station to the ship, to notify all the First Class, or 'saloon', passengers of the time of departure and for a representative of the company to travel on the train with them. The First Class passengers, naturally those occupying the highest strata of business or social life, under the escort of the firm's representative, were guided on board first.

Among the First Class passengers boarding were the Countess of Rothes; novelist Jacques Futrelle; Montreal investment banker Hudson J.C. Allison; theatrical producer Henry B. Harris; Archibald Butt, emissary and friend of President Taft; Mrs Ida Hippach of Chicago, with her daughter Jean; and Colonel Archibald Gracie.

The embarkation of the final First Class passengers, the loading of the last of the mails and the observance of certain legal formalities attending the departure were among the last items in the programme. As soon as these were completed, the signal was given for all friends to go ashore at once, and a few minutes later, the liner began her voyage. In *Titanic's* case, this was shortly after noon, accompanied by a blast on the ship's whistles.

At 12.15 p.m., the heavy mooring lines were cast off. Assisted by six tugs, *Titanic* was slowly pulled out of her berth. Upon negotiating the turn into the River Test, the tugs cast off their lines and *Titanic* proceeded under her own power, slowly picking up speed.

Proceeding down Southampton Water at a speed of 6 knots, *Titanic* drew parallel on her port side with the idle liners, *Oceanic* inside and *New York* outside, moored together at Berth 39 because of the coal strike. *Titanic's* displacement and the power of her propellers created suction that caused the line holding *New York's* stern to break free. The vessel's stern then started drifting slowly towards *Titanic*.

Opposite: Titanic's musicians. (Author's collection)

Captain Smith and Pilot George Bowyer ordered the engines stopped. Captain Gale of the tug *Vulcan* secured a line to *New York*'s stern and began to drag it away from the stationary *Titanic*. At one point, the two hulls were only 4ft apart. Two tugs then pulled *New York* away and she was secured at the edge of the Eastern Docks in the River Itchen. A collision was avoided by the narrowest of margins.

After safely navigating the Solent Channel, *Titanic* slowed to drop the pilot off before reaching the open waters of the English Channel. *Titanic* started her 68-mile journey to Cherbourg, France, while the passengers prepared for lunch, their first meal aboard.

Titanic entered Cherbourg Harbour at approximately 6.30 p.m., just before dusk. The near collision incident at Southampton caused a delayed arrival at the French port by just over an hour.

24

Letter Written by First Class Passenger Arthur Gee Aboard *Titanic*

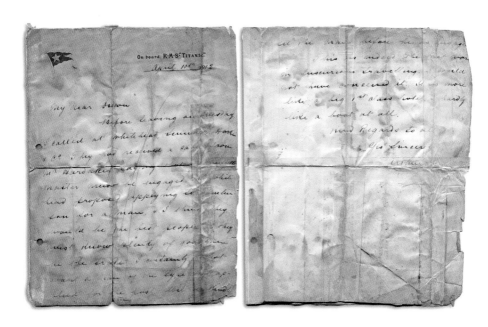

One of the First Class passengers boarding at Southampton was Arthur Gee, a manager for the firm Whitehead, Sumner, Harker & Company, merchants and exporters of Deansgate, Manchester. Arthur occupied cabin E-63, until he was relocated to a room with a porthole on 13 April.

This letter, dated 10 April 1912, was more than likely penned while en route to Cherbourg but was never posted. It was given to a fellow passenger during the sinking, who made sure it was delivered to his wife. Arthur Gee did not survive.

In 1907, White Star opened Southampton as its main transatlantic port. This decision made the port of Cherbourg accessible along the outbound route during a westward voyage. Cherbourg had a land sea wall and facilities for coastal trade, but it did not have docking facilities deep enough for ships such as *Titanic*. Because of this, *Titanic* had to anchor out in the harbour and take on the mail and passengers by tender from shore.

At the same time *Titanic* and *Olympic* were being constructed at Harland & Wolff, the two tenders *Nomadic* and *Traffic*, intended for use at Cherbourg, were built in adjoining berths. The 220.7ft-long *Nomadic* was launched on 25 April 1911, designed to carry as many as 1,000 First and Second Class passengers with their luggage. *Traffic* was launched two days later, and was a bit smaller, with a length of 175.7ft. She was intended for carrying 500 Third Class passengers and mail.

Just as the boat train left London's Waterloo station to take passengers to Southampton, a similar train called the *Train Transatlantique* departed from the Gare St-Lazare in Paris to carry passengers to Cherbourg. After a long six-hour trip aboard the train, the passengers were informed that the scheduled 4.30 p.m. boarding time for the two tenders would be delayed by at least an hour.

By 5.30 p.m., the 142 First Class and 30 Second Class passengers were allowed to board the tender *Nomadic*. The 102 Third Class passengers consisted of a mixed bunch, including some from Syria, Croatia, Armenia and other Middle Eastern nations (known as 'Continentals'), were told to board *Traffic*.

Titanic's trip across the English Channel took over four hours, travelling at 15 knots, and by the time she entered the waters of Cherbourg, the sun had started to set. At about 6.30 p.m., when the onboard passengers were having supper, *Titanic* dropped anchor and prepared for the tenders and mail.

Of the First Class passengers boarding in Cherbourg were such names as Colonel John Jacob Astor with his newly wedded wife, Madeline Force Astor, and their entourage of maids and servants; Mr and Mrs Arthur Ryerson and their three children; Omaha department store magnate Emil Brandeis; Mr Benjamin Guggenheim and his valet; Sir Cosmo Duff-Gordon and

42. - *CHERBOURG. — Les Transbordeurs, dans l'Avant-Port.*

Lady Duff-Gordon; John Borland Thayer with his wife, Marion, and their son Jack; the well-known Margaret Brown; Edith Russell and silent movie actress Dorothy Gibson.

Returning from a four-month honeymoon trip were Dickinson Bishop and his wife, Helen. Dickinson had a major share in the Round Oak Stove Company in Dowagiac, Michigan. He married Helen Walton on 7 November 1911, and they were delaying the departure from their honeymoon specifically to travel on the new *Titanic*.

Second Class notables included Baron Alfred von Drachstedt, which was an alias used by Alfred Nourney; Mr and Mrs Albert Mallet and their son; Mr and Mrs Joseph Laroche and their daughters Louise and Simonne; and American marine editor and illustrator Samuel Ward Stanton. Additionally, some fifteen First Class and nine Second Class cross-Channel passengers disembarked *Titanic* along with cargo and mails.

Observers at the time stated that *Titanic* was an impressive sight as she lay out in the water with her lights glowing against the dark sky. No photos are known to exist of *Titanic* moored at Cherbourg with her lights ablaze. Photo postcards appear to be of *Titanic* fully illuminated, but these examples are from her initial entrance into Cherbourg Harbour at about 6.30 p.m. The glow of her lights on the photo cards was created by altering the negatives.

Many passengers aboard *Titanic* spent the night of April 10 inspecting and using the facilities in their respective deck spaces

The White Star Line tender *Nomadic* (Yard No. 422) was built on slipway No. 1, alongside *Olympic* and *Titanic*, and launched by Harland & Wolff on 25 April 1911. She was initially built to transport First and Second Class passengers from Cherbourg to the *Olympic*-class ships. (Günter Bäbler collection)

The White Star Line tender *Traffic* was built to serve alongside *Nomadic* at Cherbourg to handle Third Class passengers and mails. *Traffic* (Yard No. 423) was launched on 27 April 1911 and served the White Star Line until 1927. (Günter Bäbler collection)

and public rooms, familiarising themselves with what would become their home for the next week at sea. One First Class passenger, travelling from Southampton to Queenstown, summarised his experience on *Titanic* in an article which appeared in the *Cork Constitution* on Saturday, 13 April 1912. A portion of this article read as follows:

Look how that ship is rolling. I never thought it was so rough.' The voice was a lady's, and the place was the sun deck of the Titanic. *We had just got well clear of the eastern half of the Isle of Wight and were shaping our course down the English Channel toward Cherbourg.*

The ship that had elicited the remark was a large three-masted sailing vessel which rolled and pitched so heavily that over her bow the seas were constantly breaking. But up where we were – some 60 feet above the water line – there was no indication of the strength of the tossing swell below. This indeed is the one great impression I received from my first trip on the Titanic – and everyone with whom I spoke shared it – her wonderful steadiness. Were it not for the brisk breeze blowing along the decks one would scarcely have imagined that every hour found us 20 knots further upon our course.

But other things besides her steadiness filled us with wonder. Deck over deck and apartment after apartment lent their deceitful aid to persuade us that instead of being on the sea we were still on terra firma. It is useless for me to attempt a description of the wonders of the saloon – the smoking room with its inlaid mother-of-pearl – the lounge with its green velvet and dull polished oak – the reading room with its marble fireplace and deep soft chairs and rich carpet of old rose hue – all of these things have been told over and over again, and only lose in the telling.

So vast was it all that after several hours on board some of us were still uncertain of our way about – though we must state that with commendable alacrity and accuracy some 325 found their way to the great dining saloon at 7.30 when the bugle sounded the call to dinner. After dinner, we sat in the beautiful lounge listening to the White Star orchestra playing 'The Tales of Hoffman' and 'Cavalleria Rusticana' selections, and more than once we heard the remark, 'You would never imagine you were on board a ship'. Still harder was it to believe that up on the top deck it was blowing a gale.

But we had to go to bed, and this reminds me that on the Titanic the expression is literally accurate. Nowhere were the berths of other days seen, and everywhere comfortable oaken bedsteads gave ease to the weary traveller.

Then the morning plunge in the great swimming bath, where the ceaseless ripple of the tepid sea water was almost the only indication that somewhere in the distance 72,000 horses in the guise of steam engines fretted and strained under the skilled guidance of the engineers. After the plunge a half-hour in the gymnasium helped to send one's

Titanic at
Cherbourg.
(R. Terrell
Wright
collection)

*blood coursing freely, and created a big appetite for the
morning meal.*

But if the saloon of the Titanic *is wonderful, no less so
is the second-class and in its degree the third-class. A word
from the genial Purser opened a free passage through all this
floating wonder. Lifts and lounges and libraries are not generally associated in the public mind with Second Class, yet
in the* Titanic *all are found. It needed the assurance of our
steward guide that we had left the saloon and were really in
the Second Class.*

*On the crowded third-class deck were hundreds of English,
Dutch, Italians and French mingling in happy fellowship, and
when we wandered down among them we found that to them,
too, the* Titanic *was a wonder. No more general cabins, but
hundreds of comfortable rooms with two, four or six berths
each, beautifully covered in red and white coverlets. Here, too,
are lounges and smoking rooms, less magnificent than those
amidships, to be sure, but nonetheless comfortable, and which,
with the swivel chairs and separate tables in the dining-rooms,
struck me as not quite fitting with my previous notion of steerage accommodation.*

Queenstown

The weather had remained cloudy as *Titanic* steamed towards Ireland to her final port of call at Queenstown (known as Cobh since 1920). At 11.55 a.m., *Titanic* approached the anchorage off Roche's Point, slowing to a stop and dropping anchor around 12.15 p.m. on the morning of 11 April, some 2 miles from shore.

Just as at Cherbourg, Queenstown did not have docking facilities deep enough to handle ships the size of *Titanic*. A total of 123 passengers embarked at Queenstown for the half-an-hour trip via the tenders *America* and *Ireland*: 3 First Class, 7 Second Class and 113 Third Class. Along with these passengers, *Titanic* took on 1,385 sacks of mail.

Disembarking from *Titanic* at Queenstown were eight people including a Boiler Room deserter stoker, John Coffey. Among those leaving *Titanic* were the Odell family and a theology student in the Jesuit order, Francis Browne. Browne was a teacher at Belvedere College at the time and was an avid photographer. His uncle, the Lord Bishop of Cloyne, bought him a ticket for a trip on *Titanic* from Southampton to Queenstown.

During his voyage on *Titanic*, Browne was befriended by an American millionaire couple who were seated at his table in the liner's First Class Dining Saloon. They asked him to send a

Titanic at Queenstown. (Author's collection)

message to his superior in Dublin, called the 'Provincial' of the
Jesuits, asking permission to remain on board for the remainder
of the voyage. The American couple would pay his way and for
the return trip. The message was sent, and a reply was waiting for
Browne upon his arrival in Cork Harbour consisting of the words:
'GET OFF THAT SHIP – PROVINCIAL.'

Browne left *Titanic* at Queenstown as ordered, with his camera
and negatives, having captured the maiden voyage of *Titanic*
from Southampton to Queenstown – the near accident with the
New York, the famous image of Robert D. Spedden spinning his
top on the aft end of A Deck, First Class Gymnasium instructor T.W. McCawley, passenger Jacques Futrelle, Marconi operator
Harold Bride and some of the last pictures ever taken on *Titanic*.

At 1.55 p.m. on 11 April 1912, *Titanic* weighed anchor for the last
time with 324 First Class passengers, 284 Second Class, 709 Third
Class and 891 crew aboard. The two tenders pulled away from the
ship and *Titanic* slowly turned through a half circle and steamed out
to sea. Second Class passenger Lawrence Beesley would later recall:

> In our wake soared and screamed hundreds of gulls, which
> had quarrelled and fought over the remnants of lunch pouring
> out of the waste pipes as we lay-to in the harbour entrance;
> and now they followed us in the expectation of further spoil.

All afternoon *Titanic* steamed along the south-west coast of Ireland,
bound for America and the promise of a new future for many of her
immigrants. As dusk fell, the coast disappeared astern, and the last
Titanic saw of Europe were the green hills of Eire.

The remainder of *Titanic*'s voyage was scheduled to take another
six days. She was scheduled to arrive on Wednesday, 17 April. The
crossing time was measured from the departure off the Daunt
Rock Lightvessel outside Queenstown Harbour to passing the
Ambrose Channel Lightvessel before entering New York Harbor.

With the events that occurred over the following three days
at sea, there will be much reference to ship's time. On *Titanic*, as
on other White Star Line vessels heading westward, ship's clocks
were set back each night so that at local apparent time at noon the
following day, the clocks would read 12.00. On White Star Line

vessels, this clock adjustment was done around midnight. White Star Line travel and informative booklets given to passengers on westbound voyages stated:

It is necessary to put the clock back every 24 hours. The alteration in time is made at about midnight, and the clock is usually put back from 35 to 45 minutes on each occasion, the exact amount of time depending upon the distance the ship is estimated to make by noon the next day. During the first 24 hours, however, owing to the change from Mean time to Apparent time, the alteration is likely to be considerably more than 45 minutes.

First Class passenger Frederic Spedden and his 6-year-old son, Douglas, spinning a top on the after end of A Deck. Taken on 11 April 1912, this is one of the handful of images taken by Francis Browne aboard *Titanic*. (Francis Browne/ author's collection)

The junior officers on board *Titanic* were required to keep 'watch-and-watch' with the able-bodied seamen. Third Officer Herbert Pitman was in charge of the 'port watch' and was paired with Fifth Officer Harold Lowe. Fourth Officer Joseph Boxhall was in charge of the 'starboard watch' and was paired with Sixth Officer James Moody. This meant that each watch section, port and starboard, worked four hours on and then had four hours off. To ensure that the same watch section didn't have to work the same hours every day, the four-hour period from 4 p.m. to 8 p.m. was divided into two dog watches of two hours each.

Regular sea watches for the Deck Department crew on board *Titanic*, excluding the senior officers, lookouts and those who did not have to stand regular sea watches, are shown in the table below:

Regular Sea Watches on Board Ship

First Watch	8 p.m. to Midnight
Middle Watch	Midnight to 4 a.m.
Morning Watch	4 a.m. to 8 a.m.
Forenoon Watch	8 a.m. to Noon
Afternoon Watch	Noon to 4 p.m.
First Dog Watch	4 p.m. to 6 p.m.
Second Dog Watch	6 p.m. to 8 p.m.

PART IV

THE OPEN SEA

After departing from Queenstown on 11 April, *Titanic* quickly entered the North Atlantic lane for westbound steam vessels. She began her main voyage across the Atlantic after taking departure off the Daunt Rock Lightvessel at about 2.20 p.m. GMT.* *Titanic's* path brought her around the southern coast of Ireland towards Fastnet Lighthouse. From there, she would follow the Great Circle track westbound to a location in the middle of the North Atlantic referred to as 'the corner' at 42°N, 47°W, the turning point for westbound steamers heading for the east coast of North America for that time of the year. She would then follow a rhumb line track taking her just south of the Nantucket Shoals Lightvessel, and from there to the Ambrose Channel Lightvessel, marking the arrival point and entrance to New York Harbor.

Titanic's passengers and crew settled into their daily routines for the upcoming week. Filling the corridors and great public rooms were more than 1,300 passengers, who found ways to pass their time on board. Many passengers used the open promenades on *Titanic*, some to get some exercise, walk their dogs, or just to socialise – temperature willing.

---

* Greenwich Mean Time.

25

White Star Line Deck Chair

Promenading was as much for socialising as it was for exercise and fresh air. It was de rigueur for First Class passengers and was as much about being seen as it was about seeing other people. A Deck, being sheltered and entirely reserved for First Class, was the most popular for promenading and enjoying the outdoor air on deck chairs (this deck was wide enough to permit promenading without tripping over the deck chairs arranged along the bulkheads).

Deck chairs
on *Titanic*'s
port-side
A Deck
promenade,
looking
forward.
(Author's
collection)

Overhead battens were fitted at the deck head, on which were marked numbers corresponding to numbered brass plates fastened to the chairs themselves. These numbers indicated the location of each individual chair and saved the passengers the trouble of finding their chairs when they were covered with blankets, or 'steamer rugs'.

The teak deck chairs, or 'steamer chairs', were hired at a cost of $1 or 4*s* each and were reserved before the beginning of the voyage, or from the Enquiry Office on C Deck after the ship was at sea. It was common practice for some passengers, immediately upon boarding, to reserve a deck chair in a good location.

It was not uncommon for women with daughters of a marriageable age to choose their ship on the basis of its passenger list. The purpose of this was to book passage with a rich bachelor. After embarking, the mothers would sometimes bribe the deck steward for the location of the deck chair of their intended quarry and attempt to reserve the position right next to it.

Rooms were provided on A Deck, which were fitted with shelves and lockers, well stocked with steamer rugs. These rugs, like the chairs, could be hired at least twelve hours in advance of sailing at the cost of $1 per rug for the whole voyage, or at the Enquiry Office. Stateroom pillows and blankets were not allowed on deck.

The First Class Promenade on the Boat Deck was located between the Officers' Quarters Deckhouse and the reciprocating engine casing. Promenading was a pastime in *Titanic*'s era, but the Edwardians did not like to manoeuvre around deck chairs, and serious promenaders liked to have an area reserved just for foot traffic.

A few of the passengers used the raised roof over the First Class Lounge for games, but as deck chairs were not allowed on the Boat Deck, it was summarily ignored for lounging. Deck chairs were confined to A Deck in First Class, and the after end of the Boat Deck and B Deck for Second Class. Although the occasional deck chair appears in photographs of *Olympic*'s Boat Deck, this was an exception.

Deck benches, or 'seats', as they were sometimes called, were located about the First, Second and Third Class deck areas, as well as within the engineers' and officers' promenades.

26

First Class Dining Saloon Chair

Several of *Titanic*'s Dining Room chairs were recovered after the sinking, floating in the ocean. However, none are known to exist today. This chair is from *Olympic* and is believed by historians to be identical to those on *Titanic*, including the oak frame and upholstered dark green leather.

Dining hours in the pertinent Saloons for each class of passenger were prescheduled aboard ship. *Titanic*'s First Class Dining Saloon on D Deck could seat 554 persons at one time. The Saloon doors opened at 8.00 a.m. for breakfast and continued through until 10.00 a.m. Luncheon began at 1.00 p.m., tea was at 4.00 p.m. and dinner at 7.00 p.m. Lights out in the Saloon was at 11.00 p.m. Children were not allowed to dine in First Class unless there was room, or a full fare was paid for them.

Contrary to popular belief, Captain Smith did not preside over a specific table in the Dining Saloon, though he would occasionally sit at a large, oval table located centrally in the room while at sea. The captains of ocean liners took their meals on the bridge when in pilotage waters or in dirty weather. In Captain Smith's case, he generally took his meals in his quarters, being served by his personal steward, James A. Painton.

While at sea, dinner in First Class was formal attire. However, this rule was lifted at those times when boarding or disembarking would interfere. Luncheon and dinner were announced by the ship's bugler, Peter W. Fletcher, who took his stand at different parts of the vessel in rotation. Sometimes the military call was given, but dinner was generally announced by 'The Roast Beef of Old England'. A steward in the area would also announce the commencement of mealtimes in case anyone missed the bugle call. Prior to the call for dinner, a dress call would sound about half an hour before.

A First Class dinner menu would include such entrées as sauté of chicken Lyonnaise, lamb with mint sauce and roast duckling with apple sauce, not to mention such delights as roast squab with cress or cold asparagus vinaigrette. During luncheon, First Class passengers could order from the menu, partaking of such choices as roast Surrey capon, grilled mutton chops and chicken à la Maryland, or choose from a buffet set up with dishes such as fresh lobster, Norwegian anchovies, galantine of chicken, corned ox tongue and Virginia and Cumberland ham, not to mention a selection of cheeses.

A dessert in First Class might include apple meringue, Waldorf pudding, eclairs or pastries. For breakfast, First Class had their choice of not only staples such as fresh fruit, eggs to order and

The First
Class Dining
Saloon on
board *Olympic*.
(Author's
collection)

grilled ham or sausage, but also such dishes as smoked salmon, sirloin steak and mutton chops.

Passengers were requested to sign cards when ordering wine and spirits at table, and accounts for these were then presented at the end of the voyage by the table steward or bedroom steward, to whom payment was to be made.

After supper, the passengers would disperse to other accommodations, such as the Reception Room, located at the forward end of the Dining Saloon. This accommodation served as a meeting place before meals and as a lounge afterwards. The ladies would use the Reception Room to partake in conversation over a cup of coffee or an aperitif when time would allow. For the men, smoking was allowed here at all times.

The ship's musicians played in the Reception Room at afternoon tea and from 8.00 to 9.15 p.m. As soon as the band stopped playing, the passengers would generally disperse to other areas.

Smoke Room Light Fixture

A First Class Smoke Room light fixture from *Olympic*, representing the most ornate and decorated room on *Titanic*.

The walls of the Smoke Room were fitted with ornamental, chased three-light electric wall appliqués with urn terminals and an ormolu finish. The ceiling held ornamental dull-gold scroll-pattern electroliers of three, five or nine lights with cut-glass acorn shades. Together, there were a total of thirty-nine wall appliqués and thirty-nine various ceiling lights.

The First Class Smoke Room was exclusively a retreat for the male passengers of that class, and was intended to resemble the

First Class Smoke Room on board *Olympic*. (Author's collection)

fashionable gentlemen's clubs of New York and London. Dark, carved wood and stained glass, gilded sconces, semi-private alcoves and – unique aboard the ship – a genuine coal-burning fireplace – all contributed to an atmosphere of easy relaxation, whether that involved a game of cards or just conversation over cigars or brandy. It was the most ornate and decorated room on *Titanic*.

The Smoke Room was fitted with finely carved mahogany panelling, supporting pillars and floral and scroll ornamentations with egg-and-tongue mouldings. The room's design was an adaptation of early Georgian style and was based on the style prevalent in old English houses of that period. On *Titanic*, though, the characteristic carving in the Georgian style had been largely replaced throughout by inlaid mother-of-pearl in elegant scroll and floral designs.

The coal-burning fireplace was fitted against the after bulkhead on the centre line. The mantle was of sculpted, veined marble with floral cornucopia, shell ornamentations and egg-and-tongue borders. On top of the mantle was a clock and mounted above was a painting by Norman Wilkinson entitled 'Plymouth Harbour'.

A bar with a small adjoining pantry was located aft of the Smoke Room and was shared with the Veranda and Palm Courts. This facility is where refreshments were prepared and where drinks were dispensed to the stewards. The bar and pantry facility contained cold lockers, a sink and other amenities. It was also fitted with a two-drawer Milner safe. Choice brands of cigars, cigarettes and tobacco could be purchased, hence the need for the safe as money was transferred.

The First Class Smoke Room opened at 8.00 a.m. and the lights were extinguished at midnight. Passengers were requested not to engage in 'high play' or use objectionable language and were also cautioned to be vigilant against the predations of the professional gamblers who frequented the transatlantic liners.

28

First Class Lounge Light Sconce

An existing light sconce from *Olympic*'s First Class Lounge. The majority of oak panelling and most of the wall sconces were bought at an auction of *Olympic*'s fittings in 1935 and remain intact at the White Swan Hotel in Alnwick, Northumberland. *Olympic*'s lounge panels were nearly identical to those of *Titanic*.

The First Class Lounge on board *Olympic*. (Author's collection)

A section of *Titanic*'s First Class Lounge panelling was retrieved from the ocean after the sinking and exists to this day. The intricate carving of the wreckage panel is only slightly different to the matching piece at the White Swan Hotel. All of the carved woodwork on *Titanic* and *Olympic* was done by hand and no two pieces are exact as they would be if made by machine.

The owner of the White Swan, when purchasing the lounge panels in 1935, also bought the ceiling lights of the First Class Smoke Room. The '*Olympic* Suite' at the White Swan, therefore, is an amalgamation of *Olympic*'s lounge wall panels with the Smoke Room ceiling lights. The reason why the pieces were mixed is unknown.

The First Class Lounge ceiling lights consist of specially designed electroliers, the largest of which was located in the centre of the room on the ship and exists to this day at Cutlers' Hall, in Sheffield, England.

Titanic's First Class Lounge was located on A Deck and was arguably one of the most elegant rooms in the ship – a period source described *Olympic*'s as 'a magnificent salon, pronounced by many persons the finest room ever built into a ship. It is more suggestive of a state apartment in a palace than a room on shipboard.' The detailing of this room – designed in the noble Louis XV style – was taken from the French Palace at Versailles. The same source said, with obvious approval:

> *The pure marble fireplace, with glowing grate beneath, various large recesses at the side of the room, with broad-paned windows; spacious couches eloquent of comfort, and numerous small tables for cards or tea, give the great room an air of completeness that one associates most readily with magnificent buildings on shore.*

The room was panelled throughout in the finest English oak, with finely carved *boiseries* of scrolled floral and shell ornamentation. The Lounge was carpeted with green and gold, which were also the dominant colours in the furniture upholstery. At the forward end of the room was an electric fireplace, and at the after end was a large mahogany bookcase, concave in shape to fit the curved wall against which it stood.

29

À La Carte Restaurant Receipt

WHITE STAR LINE.   No.

R.M.S. "TITANIC"

Voyage No. _____ 191

Name of Passenger _____

No. of Ticket _____ No. of Persons _____

Received *from the Purser the sum of £* _____

rebate for taking meals in the Restaurant.

Passenger's Signature _____

First Class passengers on *Titanic* were given an option with their tickets to take their meals at any time of the day in the À La Carte Restaurant on B Deck. This option would earn the passenger a maximum £5 rebate on the ticket price but would require the passenger to pay a bill at the end of the voyage and eating in the Dining Saloon would no longer be available to them. The artefact pictured here was a rebate receipt issued by the Purser if the decision to take meals exclusively in the restaurant was announced after boarding.

Among the hundreds of First Class passengers carried on every voyage there were always a number who requested food service at unusual hours or inconvenient times, and if their wants, however unreasonable, were not immediately attended to, they were likely to complain about the inattention of the ship's staff. To satisfy these requests meant that the stewards and cooks were delayed

The First Class À La Carte Restaurant on board *Olympic*. (Author's collection)

from serving other passengers, and if an à la carte restaurant could be created to satisfy their needs and wants, then the service in the Dining Saloon would not suffer. It was also foreseen that a restaurant would appeal to that group of passengers who might want to take their meals at special times (when the Dining Saloon was closed). And, by offering a restaurant, the Dining Saloon would not always be filled to capacity and the pressure on the stewards there would be relaxed somewhat, to the benefit of the passengers.

Titanic's À La Carte Restaurant was located on B Deck and was open at 8.00 a.m. serving food until 11.00 p.m. It was a great convenience to those whose appetites were not equal to sampling all the courses that constituted a dinner in the Dining Saloon. The restaurant was widely admired as a beautiful room, and many people thought meals here were preferable to those in the Dining Saloon.

One of the chief attractions of the À La Carte restaurant was that a passenger could get anything they wanted at any time. If they felt hungry after a game of quoits or a turn around the deck, they could go to the restaurant and have something to appease their hunger until the next regular meal. Another advantage of the restaurant was that if the passenger did not want anything between the soup course and dessert, they could skip the intervening courses and go right from one to the other.

The style of decoration adopted for the restaurant was that of the Louis XVI period. The room was panelled from floor to ceiling in French walnut of a light fawn colour, the mouldings and ornaments being richly carved and gilded. At the forward end of the restaurant was a buffet with a top of *fleur de pêche* marble, supported by panelling and plaster matching the design of the wall panels.

The adjoining Café Parisian was intended to give the appearance of a French pavement café. The long, narrow dimensions of this space, coupled with large, rectangular windows and trained ivy and other plants climbing the trellis-work panelling, worked to further this illusion. Small groups of tables and chairs were arranged along the inner and outer walls, and passengers could be served meals and light refreshments here between 8.00 a.m. and 11.00 p.m.

At the B Deck landing of the aft First Class staircase was the Reception Room for the À La Carte Restaurant and Café Parisien. The Reception Room was provided for friends and parties to meet prior to taking their seats in the restaurant, and later, to gather socially after dinner. Music was provided by a trio of string musicians.

Although *The Shipbuilder* suggested that the Reception Room was decorated in Georgian style, it was really a combination of period styles. The mahogany panels of the room were indeed carried out in Georgian style and painted white, but the oak staircase was in William and Mary style. With its Louis XIV balustrades and bronze cherub, it was the central feature of the room.

The À La Carte Restaurant was managed by Signor Luigi Gatti, who was originally from Oddenino's Imperial Restaurant in London. Gatti had accepted the commission from the White Star Line to run *Titanic*'s restaurant as a concession. The restaurant staff, including the cashier clerks, were considered outsiders by the rest of the crew as they were brought on by the restaurant manager and were not under control of the Chief Steward.

30

Second Class Dining Room Chair

This Second Class Dining Saloon chair from a White Star ship is nearly identical to those used on *Titanic*, where Second Class passengers ate at long cafeteria-style tables. The room was fitted with carved, oak-framed chairs on a cast-iron support, just as in this example. As with nearly all of the chairs on a ship of this era, they were secured in position with bolts and could not move, although they could swivel on the spot.

Second Class passengers were called to meals with a gong, and although the fare was not as lavish as in First Class, they would be quite satisfied with their choices of food. Breakfast was much the same as in First Class. The luncheon offerings would contain such items as pea soup, spaghetti au gratin, corned beef, vegetable dumplings, roast mutton, potatoes, cold cuts and side dishes.

For dinner, Second Class passengers could choose from dishes such as baked haddock, curried chicken and rice, spring lamb and roast turkey, accompanied by vegetables and potatoes – plainer fare than in First Class, to be sure, but of the same quality (it was prepared in the same galley, for that matter).

Second Class mealtimes were much the same as First Class, adjusted for two sittings if needed during the busy season. Having two sittings also cut down on the work for the staff as the combined First and Second Class Galley served both dining saloons. The Second Class Dining Saloon had 394 seats, but on this voyage there was only need for some 284 passengers. Breakfast was served at 8.00 a.m., luncheon at 12.30 p.m., dinner at 6.30 p.m. with tea being served at the traditional 4.00 p.m.

Third Class began their day with the ringing of the breakfast gong at 7.30 a.m. At 8.00 a.m., the gong was rung again, announcing that breakfast was served. A second seating commenced at 9.00 a.m. This was needed because the Third Class Dining Saloon had only 473 seats and carried 709 passengers. When breakfast was finished, the passengers proceeded to the open decks or the public rooms while the stewards cleaned their cabins. At 11.00 a.m. the women and children received bouillon (a thin soup or broth). Dinner was held at noon and 1.00 p.m. and tea at 5.00 p.m. and 6.00 p.m.

Olympic's
Second Class
Dining Saloon.
(Author's
collection)

Titanic's Third Class Dining Saloon was provided with tables covered with white cloths. Each place was set with a knife, fork and spoon. Bread, salt, pepper and mustard were set along the centres of the tables. Soup and meat were served from the pantry; vegetables, preserves, pickles and sugar were placed at either end of the table in large dishes and each passenger could serve themselves.

The Third Class menus indicated the assortment of dishes for all meals on a particular day for the whole voyage. This is different to the First and Second Class Dining Saloons, in which separate menus were provided for each meal. A Third Class bill of fare for one sitting is as follows:

Breakfast at Eight O'Clock. – Oatmeal Porridge and Milk, Tea, Coffee, Sugar, Milk, Fresh Bread and Butter, Herrings, Potatoes, Ling Fish and Egg Sauce, or Irish Stew, according to the day of the week.

Dinner at One O'Clock. – Soup, Beef, Mutton, Carrots and Turnips, Green Peas, Pork or Ling Fish and Sauce, with Bread and Potatoes, Plum Pudding, Rice Pudding, Stewed Apples and Rice, or Stewed Prunes and Rice, according to the day of the week.

Tea at Six O'Clock. – Tea, Sugar, Milk, Fresh Bread and Butter, Jam or Cheese, and Pickles, Corned Beef Hash, or Tinned Beef, according to the day of the week. Oatmeal Gruel was available at eight o'clock.

Note. – For Women and Children – Chicken Broth or Beef Tea daily at eleven o'clock, and Tea, Coffee and Milk at all hours.

Olympic's Third Class Dining Saloon. (Author's collection)

31

Turkish Bath Ticket

No. 601

WHITE   STAR   LINE.

R.M.S.   " TITANIC."

This ticket entitles bearer to use of Turkish or Electric Bath on one occasion.

Paid 4/- or 1 Dollar.

First Class passengers on *Titanic* were provided with a Turkish Bath facility on F Deck forward. The facility was open to ladies between 10 a.m. and 1 p.m., and gentlemen from 2 to 6 p.m. The Purser sold tickets at the C Deck Enquiry Office for $1 (4s). Pictured here is an example of a *Titanic* Turkish Bath ticket. It has been stated that a small number of the tickets came off *Titanic* with survivors, but of the artefacts that appear in auctions or are held in private collections (some curiously still with the book stub), it is unknown if any are authentic.

Most, if not all, of the big liners of *Titanic*'s era provided space for passengers to exercise or pass their time with what, in modern times, would be considered leisure facilities. The Turkish Bath was only one part of the fitness accommodations for First Class passengers on *Titanic*. The Gymnasium, adjacent to the First Class entrance on the Boat Deck, was open concurrently with the baths, and to children only between 1 and 3 p.m. It was equipped with both traditional exercise equipment and what were considered in 1912 to be the latest electric exercise appliances. For traditional recreation, the passenger could enjoy devices such as clubs, a pair of grips and a punching bag, although gloves and foils were not allowed.

The Gymnasium's electrically powered machines were supplied by Rossel, Schwarz & Co. of Wiesbaden, Germany. They consisted of one abdomen-rubbing machine, one back-rubbing machine, one trunk-rotating machine (electric camel), two horse-riding machines – one outfitted with an English saddle for the gentlemen and one outfitted with an English side-saddle for ladies, both of which were driven by the same electric motor – and a height-measuring machine. The latter was a device that measured height by means of a lifted conveyance using an electric motor.

The Gymnasium offered other non-electric Sandow exercisers, which were regarded as beneficial and were, no doubt, an interesting and amusing diversion for passengers with time on their hands. In the forward port corner, next to the oak picture case, were two bicycle-racing machines, supplied by Spencer, Heath & George Ltd. With this apparatus, an oversized wall dial was mounted to the bulkhead, indicating the speed and distance in yards travelled for each bicycle. The bicycles were mounted side by side, facing the dial, which allowed passengers to race each other.

Located forward on G Deck, next to the Post Office, was the Squash and Racquet Ball Court. Tickets could be reserved at the Enquiry Office at 50 cents (2s) per half an hour. This included equipment and the services of the professional, in this case Fred Wright.

A staircase along the starboard side of the court descended from the First Class area on E Deck, with another staircase on the other side continuing down to the playing level on G Deck. The passageway between the two at the F Deck level, on the after side of the court, served as a spectators' gallery.

Passenger Archibald Gracie would later recall:

I enjoyed myself as if I were in a summer palace on the seashore, surrounded with every comfort – there was nothing to indicate or suggest that we were on the stormy Atlantic Ocean. The motion of the ship and the noise of its machinery were scarcely discernible on deck or in the saloons, either day or night. But when Sunday morning came, I considered it high time to begin my customary exercises, and determined for the rest of the voyage to patronize the squash racquet court, the gymnasium, the swimming pool, etc. I was up early before breakfast and met the professional racquet player in a half hour's warming up, preparatory for a swim in the six foot deep tank of salt water, heated to a refreshing temperature. In no swimming bath had I ever enjoyed such pleasure before.

32

Blank Writing Paper with *Titanic* Letterhead and Envelope

Blank paper with the ship's name on the letterhead was a common item offered free of charge to passengers. Paper and envelopes were made available to all classes for writing to one's family, friends and associates. The owners of the line hoped that the words written about the passenger's experiences aboard would be positive, and hence the ship's name at the top acted as free advertising. This practice is still undertaken to this day, on land and sea.

Each class of passengers was provided space to promenade and designated specific areas for entertainment. For those in First Class wanting private and quiet time, the Reading and Writing Room, on A Deck adjacent to the First Class Lounge, was open daily from 8 a.m. to 11.30 p.m. This room was set up, exactly as it was named, for reading and writing.

It was a spacious room with a tall ceiling. Large windows admitted abundant amounts of natural light and contributed to the spacious appearance of the room, with the uppermost windows being clerestory, extending through the deck above. On the port side of the room was a great bow window with a radius of 18ft.

The furniture consisted of settees and tables with chairs for reading. For writing, there were four double-sided tables, each fitted with a lamp and stationery holder in the centre where blank letterhead stationery and envelopes were provided.

The Veranda Café and Palm Court, aft on A Deck, was a room divided in half by a Second Class staircase trunk. Here, one could order light refreshments. It was glass enclosed and provided a sense of being open to the air while providing a panoramic view of the ocean. The port side of the Veranda and Palm Court was directly connected to the First Class Smoke Room and was used primarily by the men, while the women and children generally occupied the starboard side.

Second Class passengers had facilities that were just below the level of First Class in way of décor. A library, aft on C Deck, and Smoking Room, just above on B Deck, were flanked by covered deck space on which passengers could promenade.

Third Class passengers had their own open deck spaces forward and aft. On C Deck, just below the Poop Deck, they had a general

room with a piano and a smoking room for card and domino games. Both rooms were fitted with tables, chairs and benches.

All three classes of Passenger were advised by steamship companies to not venture outside of their specific areas. It was First and Second Class that this statement was particularly aimed at, as they were at times observed sight-seeing in Third Class, and risked contracting disease or other illness that may cause undue delay by the health officials at New York. The barrier between the First and Second Class passengers was less rigid than that between Second and Third. Because the Second Class compartments were exceedingly comfortable, more so than the accommodations of many steamers only a few years before, this tempted many to 'travel second' who would otherwise 'travel first'. There was also the difference in fares, which to many people was worth considering, and the fact that certain established conventions – such as dressing formally for dinner – were not observed in Second Class.

It occasionally happened that First and Second Class passengers were acquainted, and in that case, no resentment was felt if the First Class passenger entered a Second Class area to chat with his friend. On a North Atlantic liner, it was possible for a First Class passenger to invite a Second Class passenger to lunch with

Passengers in the First Class Reading and Writing Room aboard *Olympic* in the 1920s. The room was the same as on *Titanic* but was renamed the Drawing Room. (From an original White Star Line publicity film/author's collection)

him in the À La Carte Restaurant, if the ship had one, upon payment of a substantial fee for the privilege. However, the practice was generally objected to, as it was often abused. Under no circumstances whatsoever could a Third Class passenger visit a First Class area, and social conventions at the time would have made any such invitation extremely unlikely in any case.

One myth that persists to this day is that of locked gates extending from floor to ceiling between the Third Class areas and the rest of the ship. Although segregation of emigrants was required by United States Immigration Law in order to prevent the spread of infectious diseases, this was accomplished far more effectively by the existing social barriers than any other means.

Vertically folding gates and other physical forms of separation were in place at various locations throughout the *Titanic*, but their primary purpose was to clearly mark points through which Third Class passengers could not pass, as many could not read. Gates were not intended, nor were they constructed, as a means of forcible confinement or physical restriction.

There were a few instances where Third Class passengers found themselves behind vertical gated barriers during the evacuation of *Titanic*. This was due to the fact that these passengers, who were not given direction by a staff member, were not using their intended exit route.

33

'Honour and Glory Crowning Time'

'Honour and Glory Crowning Time' recreated in full scale by Alan St George, founder of titanicclock.com. Alan painstakingly researched the piece and recreated it using oak, composition material and resin with faux graining to blend it all together.

A view over the railing from *Olympic*'s Boat Deck First Class entrance foyer, looking down at the half-landing of the Grand Staircase with the 'Honour and Glory' carving in view. (Author's collection)

The First Class Entrance Hall on the Boat Deck was designed to serve as a gallery to look down upon the Grand Staircase that is so well known among *Titanic* enthusiasts. The half-landing between the Boat Deck and A Deck was ornamented with a detailed carving representing 'Honour and Glory Crowning Time', which was sculpted originally for *Titanic* by Charles Wilson in English oak.

The inspiration for this piece dates to 1800 and is from the Palace of the Tuileries in Paris. There, in the Louis XIV Salon, was the beautiful clock by sculptor Auguste-Marie Taunay. Unfortunately, Taunay's clock was destroyed by fire in 1871. However, *Olympic*'s version of Wilson's famous clock survives at the Sea City Museum in Southampton.

The piece consists of the allegorical figure of Honour, exalted by the palm-bearing Glory. Long before the palm leaf became a Christian symbol, it was used by the ancient Romans to represent victory and triumph. In ancient Greece, laurel wreaths were awarded to victors in athletic competitions, including the ancient Olympics. Laurels symbolised victory, and in Rome they were used to crown triumphant commanders.

It has been thought that the laurel wreath in the *Olympic*-class ships' 'Honour and Glory' panels first crowned Glory's head, from where she removed it and laid it down against the pedestal supporting the timepiece, thus, in effect, 'Crowning Time'. Of course, the laurel leaf motif was found elsewhere on the ship, and in particular, it was featured on the handrails of the fore and aft First Class staircases. Honour is shown recording on a tablet this important moment in history, when Western civilisation literally dominated the world of trade, transportation and technology.

In Victorian and Edwardian monumental sculpture, these classical symbols of victory, success and honour were used so routinely there was no doubt that the meaning was quite clearly understood by a public more accustomed to its symbology than we are today. It was certainly perfectly at home with the First Class passengers.

The globe under Honour's foot has etched longitudinal and latitudinal lines with land masses and a line showing the North Atlantic route of the White Star Line's ships from the United Kingdom to the United States.

PART V

VOYAGE INTO HISTORY

34

First Class Cut-Glass Electrolier

These gilded cut-glass electroliers were used in the area of the Grand Staircase aboard *Titanic* and *Olympic*. A more decorative version consisting of threaded glass beads, termed a 'jewelled basket', was used specifically in the Grand Staircase entrance foyers on the Boat and A Decks, while this cut-glass version was used on all other decks except D Deck.

In 1986, when Dr Robert Ballard explored the gaping hole in *Titanic*'s wreck where the First Class Grand Staircase once existed, he observed a number of the jewelled basket lights still hanging from the deck head by the electric wiring that once powered them. Subsequent dives, which explored the interior of *Titanic*, have taken images of these ghostly hanging-basket electroliers as well as the cut-glass version pictured here. They are haunting, and remind us that luxury and elegance once existed here among the debris and rusticles.

This artefact was chosen to lead us into the pertinent historic events leading up the night of 14 April 1912.

Friday, 12 April and Saturday, 13 April were uneventful days at sea with passengers carrying on in their routines. First and Second Class passengers would have traversed the decks via their main staircases or the contingent elevators. No doubt First Class passengers spent time in the beautiful Grand Staircase foyers at the Boat and A Decks under the iron-decorated elliptical glass dome with fifty-light chandelier; the dome being illuminated by skylights during the day and artificially at night.

Third Class used their promenades and public rooms during the day. After tea was served in the evening, they again took to the public rooms or generally to the Third Class open space on D Deck forward at the bow. It was in this location where the passengers provided their own entertainment with music, singing, dancing and a generally convivial atmosphere.

At 10.30 a.m. on each day of the voyage, except Sunday, Captain Smith, the ship's surgeon and certain department heads made an inspection of the vessel. The group of officers strode throughout the ship, examining, observing and noting the sanitary conditions from deck to deck.

At noon, the Captain was on the bridge to confer with his deck officers with regard to the daily navigational readings. With sextants in hand, they proceeded to 'shoot the sun', which calculated the vessel's position. Shortly afterwards, the officers compared readings and the determination of the ship's position was logged and then posted in the main companionways and Smoke Rooms of each class. The determination of the ship's daily position allowed for the calculation of the distance travelled since the previous day's reading.

A number of First Class passengers recalled looking at *Titanic*'s daily progress in the A Deck companionway, which was located adjacent to the Grand Staircase. This may have been presented in the form of a chart of the Atlantic Ocean within a carved frame, with the ship's noontime position being marked on the chart each day.

It was, and still is to this day, a common practice to post a ship's daily run on a chart of the route located at some central point in the ship. In the days of the great Atlantic liners, passengers would frequently place wagers predicting the ship's run on any given day.

Titanic's daily run from Thursday to Friday was 484 miles, Friday to Saturday, 519 miles, and Saturday to noon on Sunday, 546 miles. There was talk among passengers that on this maiden voyage, the White Star Line wished to set a crossing record, and additional boilers had been fired up early on Sunday morning, anticipating this increase in speed with the possibility of arriving late on Tuesday, 16 April.

Titanic had enough coal and could very well have beaten the crossing time record of her older sister *Olympic* – from light vessel to light vessel. However, International Mercantile Marine regulations stated that ships were not to dock prior to Wednesday in New York. Among the logistical needs of the terminal facilities, many passengers had arranged for transportation from White Star's Pier 59 on Wednesday, not Tuesday.

Twenty-four of the twenty-nine boilers were lit on Sunday in anticipation of an increase in speed on Monday. This was surely to allow *Titanic*'s engineers and the Harland & Wolff Guarantee Group representatives a chance to study the effects of a full-speed run at load draught. One of the factors they would have been interested in would be any excessive vibration caused by the propellers at varying revolutions of the shafts. *Titanic* could achieve 22 knots, perhaps 23. At 75 revolutions per minute, the propellers drove *Titanic* through the water at 21½ knots, or almost 24¾ land miles per hour.

Those aboard *Titanic* who wished to utilise the Marconi wireless services went to the Enquiry Office on C Deck. Handwritten messages were paid for at the desk, at a predetermined rate per word. The message was then sent via pneumatic tube to the Marconi operator's desk. Incoming messages were handwritten on paper by the operator and then typed out on a Marconi letterhead before being sent down to the Enquiry Office for delivery via a bell boy to the passenger. Messages regarding navigation were taken directly to the bridge, which was a short distance and in the same deckhouse as the Marconi Room.

Titanic had received many wireless messages of congratulations and good wishes for a successful maiden voyage on Friday morning. These came from a host of other ships, some also including notice of ice sightings. This was not uncommon for April crossings.

From Friday into Saturday, eastbound and westbound vessels travelling along the North Atlantic lanes were encountering ice near the parallel of 41° 50' N latitude. Some of the vessels reported ice via their wireless systems, while other ships not so equipped reported the ice upon arrival at their respective ports:

```
Ice had been seen between 41° and 42° North,
and between 49° and 50° West .. Field ice, some
growlers, some bergs ..
```

The Morning Watch on Sunday, 14 April began at 4.00 a.m.* Third Officer Herbert Pitman and Fifth Officer Harold Lowe replaced Fourth Officer Joseph Boxhall and Sixth Officer James Moody. Lookouts Frederick Fleet and Reginald Lee relieved lookouts Archibald 'Archie' Jewell and George Symons.

Below, in the Engine and Boiler Room spaces, both Junior Second Engineer Norman Harrison and Junior Assistant Second Engineer Herbert Harvey took up their watches. They relieved William Farquharson and Bertie Wilson.

Second Officer Charles Lightoller replaced Chief Officer Henry Wilde at 6.00 a.m. as Officer of Watch, while lookouts Alfred Evans and George Hogg replaced lookouts Frederick Fleet and Reginald Lee. At about this time, the ballast and freshwater tanks were sounded by the carpenter in accordance with IMM rules.

The Forenoon Watch began at 8.00 a.m. Fourth Officer Joseph Boxhall and Sixth Officer James Moody replaced Third Officer

*   All times are now apparent ship's time unless otherwise noted.

Pitman and Fifth Officer Lowe. Lookouts Archibald Jewell and George Symons relieved Alfred Evans and George Hogg in the crow's nest. During this time, *Titanic*'s three remaining double-ended boilers were lit up in Boiler Room No. 2 in anticipation of a speed increase the following day.

Chief Engineer Bell reported that the coal fire that had burned continuously in Boiler Room No. 6 since *Titanic*'s sea trials, almost two weeks earlier, had been extinguished shortly after noon. Coal fires were caused by spontaneous combustion of the coal and were not uncommon in this era, before the wide use of fuel oil to heat the boilers. The smouldering coal, which was at the bottom of the pile within a bunker, had to be uncovered by manually removing the coal on top and moving it to another location. Once the smouldering coal was exposed, it was extinguished.

At 9.00 a.m. on Sunday, 14 April, *Titanic* received a wireless transmission from *Caronia*, eastbound from New York to Liverpool via Queenstown:

```
Captain, Titanic - West-bound steamers report
bergs growlers and field ice in 42° N, from
49° to 51° W, April 12. Compliments, Barr.
```

The message was delivered to Captain Smith on the bridge, who posted it for his officers to read and note. *Titanic* replied to *Caronia*:

```
Thanks for message and information. Have had
variable weather throughout - Smith.
```

The reported ice was 300 miles to *Titanic*'s south-east.

Non-denominational worship services using the White Star Line Prayer Book, no doubt based on the Book of Common Prayer of the Church of England, were offered for each class of passenger on White Star ships. If the complement of passengers included clergymen from other denominations, they were offered an opportunity to conduct services for passengers within their respective areas of the ship. The Captain led the service for First Class, while the Second and Third Class Pursers were in charge of the Divine Service for their respective classes of passengers.

On *Titanic*, Divine Service for First Class passengers was held at 10.30 a.m., led by Captain Smith. The service was carried out from the White Star Line Prayer Book and was concluded by 11.15 a.m. In Second Class, the service was led by Second Purser Reginald Barker, reading from the more traditional Church of England book. The music for the hymns was played by the ship's musicians.

First Class passenger Archibald Gracie recalled:

> *On Sunday morning, April 14th, this marvellous ship, the perfection of all vessels hitherto conceived by the brain of man, had, for three and one-half days, proceeded on her way from Southampton to New York over a sea of glass, so level it appeared, without encountering a ripple brought on the sur-face of the water by a storm … The exercise and the swim gave me an appetite for a hearty breakfast. Then followed the church service in the dining saloon, and I remember how much I was impressed with the 'Prayer for those at Sea', also the words of the hymn, which we sang, No. 418 of the Hymnal.*

A Divine Service was offered in Third Class by their head steward. There were, however, three Catholic priests aboard, travelling in Second Class. These men were allowed to offer their services to Catholic passengers. Each day, Father Juozas Montvila attended to the Third Class, while Father Thomas Byles and Father Josef Peruschitz offered up their services elsewhere if needed. Each handled spoken mass daily in both Third and Second Class. On Sunday morning, Father Thomas Byles celebrated mass in the Second Class Library and recited the rosary for many passengers in Third Class on Sunday afternoon. On Sunday morning, Father Peruschitz went to the steerage area, where he heard confessions, celebrated mass and administered Holy Communion.

At 11:20 a.m., a message was received from the SS *Noordam* by way of *Coronia*:

```
Captain SS Titanic. Congratulations on new
command. Had moderate westerly winds, fair
weather, no fog. Much ice reported in lat. 42°
24' to 42° 45' N and long. 49° 50' to 50° 20'
W. Compliments. Krol.
```

At noon, the Captain and officers gathered to shoot the sun and confirmed 546 miles had been covered over the previous twenty-four hours. The average speed for the third day's run was 22 knots, with the revolutions kept at 75–76.

At 1.42 p.m. a wireless message from *Baltic*, eastbound from New York to Liverpool via Queenstown, was received:

```
Captain Smith, Titanic — Have had moderate
variable winds and clear fine weather since
leaving. Greek steamer 'Athenai' reports
passing icebergs and large quantities of
field ice today in lat. 41° 51'N., long.
49° 52'W .. Wish you and 'Titanic' all success.
— Commander.
```

The message was delivered to Captain Smith as he conversed with J. Bruce Ismay. Smith handed the copy of the message to Ismay, who put it in his pocket. Ismay would take it with him and later show the message to several passengers. Sometime around 7.15 p.m., Smith asked for the message back from Ismay so that it could be put in the Chart Room.

At 1.45 p.m. a message from the liner *Amerika* to the United States Hydrographic Office at Washington DC was received and relayed to *Titanic*'s wireless operator:

```
Amerika passed two large icebergs in 41° 27'
N, 50° 8' W on April 14.
```

This message was not sent to *Titanic*'s bridge.

By 3.00 p.m. *Titanic* was making close to 22.3 knots through the water. Third Officer Pitman and Fifth Officer Lowe were relieved by Fourth Officer Boxhall and Sixth Officer Moody at 4.00 p.m. This turn of watch was known as 'The First Dogwatch'. In the crow's nest, Frederick Fleet and Reginald Lee relieved lookouts Archie Jewell and George Symons.

At 5.20 p.m. *Titanic* reached what was termed 'The Corner'. This was the point where westbound ships usually altered their course. However, Captain Smith decided to delay this bearing change for thirty minutes. Therefore, the ship's course was altered at 5.50 p.m. from S 62° W to S 85° W. This alteration would place *Titanic's* course slightly to the south and west of what would have been the normal course. The deck officers believed this was done by Smith to avoid the ice that had been previously reported.

A change in weather was noticed by passengers at about 5.30 p.m. The temperature was dropping rapidly, and many people left the outer decks for the interior rooms. Between 5.30 and 7.30 p.m., the air temperature dropped by 10 degrees to 33°F. Second Officer Lightoller, who relieved Chief Officer Wilde on the bridge at 6.00 p.m., ordered the carpenter to sound the ballast and water tanks to ascertain if they had started freezing.

First Officer Murdoch took over at 7.00 p.m. as Officer of the Watch to allow Lightoller to take dinner. It was about this time that the double-ended boilers, which were lit earlier in the morning, were brought into use.

At 7.20 p.m., First Officer Murdoch ordered Lamp Trimmer Samuel Hemming, 'Hemming, when you go forward see the fore-scuttle hatch closed, as we are in the vicinity of ice, and there is a glow coming from that, and I want everything dark before the bridge'.* When Lightoller returned from his break at 7.30, Murdoch reported the falling temperature to him.

---

*   Murdoch was speaking of placing the covers over the skylights on the hatch cover of No. 1 Hold. Light was showing from the 3rd Class Open Space on the deck below. Blocking out light was needed in order to preserve the 'night eyes' of those in the crow's nest and the officers on the bridge. It was necessary to darken any place at the forward part of the ship that would affect their eyes when adjusting in and out of light. For this purpose, the bulkhead lights forward of the First Class entrance on the Boat Deck had blocking shields to keep the light from projecting forward.

35

À La Carte Restaurant Serviette Ring

Captain Smith attended a private party in the À La Carte Restaurant, given by Mr and Mrs George D. Widener, with guests including the Thayers, the Carters, Major Archibald Butt, and their son, Harry. This specially designed napkin, or serviette, ring is from *Olympic*'s À La Carte Restaurant. It is identical to examples known to be on *Titanic*.

While the Captain was having supper with the Wideners in the restaurant on B Deck, a wireless message from *Californian* to *Antillian* was overheard by *Titanic*:

```
To Captain, Antillian: Six thirty pm, appar-
ent ship's time; lat. 42° 3' N, long 49° 9' W.
Three large bergs 5 miles to the southward of
us. Regards, Lord.
```

Harold Bride took the message to one of the officers on the bridge, but he could not recall which one he handed it to.

Captain Smith returned to the bridge just before 9.00 p.m. and had a conversation with Lightoller, discussing the weather. Lightoller would later describe the conversation:

We commenced speaking about the weather. He said, 'There is not much wind.' I said, 'No, it is a flat calm.' I said that it was a pity the wind had not kept up with us whilst we were going through the ice region. Of course he knew I meant the water ripples breaking on the base of the berg ... I remember saying, 'of course there will be a certain amount of reflected light from the bergs', with which the Captain agreed. Even with the blue side toward us, we both agreed that there would still be the white outline.

Captain Smith retired at about 9.20 p.m. His last words to Lightoller were, 'If it becomes at all doubtful let me know at once. I shall be just inside.' Lightoller would then send a message to the crow's nest to 'keep a sharp lookout for ice, particularly small ice and growlers, until daylight'.

At 9.40 p.m. a message was received in *Titanic*'s wireless room:

```
From Mesaba to Titanic. In latitude 42° N to
41° 25', longitude 49° W to longitude 50° 30'
W. saw much heavy pack ice and great number
large icebergs, also field ice, weather
good, clear.
```

This message never reached *Titanic*'s bridge. Harold Bride had turned in for a nap, and Phillips was alone and busy with commercial traffic with the Cape Race shore station.

36

Quartermaster Alfred Olliver's Silver Pocket Watch

On the night of 14 April 1912, Alfred Olliver had been at the wheel on *Titanic*'s bridge until 10 p.m., at which time he was relieved by Robert Hichens. Olliver then became the standby quartermaster and was running messages from the officers and doing other errands when he heard the three bells ring out from the crow's nest. This silver pocket watch was with him on *Titanic*. Olliver survived in Lifeboat No.5.

At 10.00 p.m., Second Officer Lightoller was relieved by First Officer Murdoch. Lightoller passed on Captain Smith's instructions and advised the Captain would be just inside his quarters if needed. Lookouts Jewell and Symons were replaced by Fleet and Lee, and Quartermaster Robert Hichens replaced Alfred Olliver at the wheel in the Wheelhouse.

Since 8.00 p.m., *Titanic* had travelled 45 nautical miles and was now making some 22.5 knots. Unknown to Murdoch, as the message wasn't passed along, the SS *Californian* had been forced to stop because of field ice directly in her path. Captain Lord of the *Californian* directed Cyril Evans, the ship's radio operator, to advise any vessels in the vicinity that they had stopped for the night:

```
Titanic: MGY this is MWL. We are stopped and
surrounded by ice.
```

Phillips, on *Titanic*, was busy working Cape Race at the time and told Evans to 'Shut up. I am busy. I am working Cape Race' [or 'DDD'].*

Lookouts Fleet and Lee came on duty at 10.00 p.m. At 11.30, almost half an hour before they would be relieved, a slight haze had appeared directly ahead. Despite being 50ft above the level of the Fo'c'sle Deck, the men still had trouble focusing on what was ahead in the haze.

Within seconds, Fleet realised that what they were seeing was an iceberg. He rang the bell three times, which was the signal for an object directly ahead, and reached into the box containing the telephone. Sixth Officer Moody answered, and Fleet shouted out, 'Are you there?'

'Yes. What do you see?'

'Iceberg right ahead.'

'Thank you.'

---

* The letter 'D' was the Marconi code to indicate urgency. The continuous tapping of the letter 'D' was an abbreviation used by Marconi wireless operators to advise another to stop interrupting the transmission – in effect, 'shut up', although Phillips did not physically tap out 'shut up'.

Fleet and Lee braced themselves for impact. The berg was approaching just off the port bow. It was taller than the Fo'c'sle but below the level of the crow's nest. No white could be seen – just black – but as the bow scraped along the side of the ice, the lookouts could see a glimmer of white. It was not until the berg passed the forward Well Deck that the white colour could be seen.

Fleet and Lee could feel the bow crushing the ice and hear the grinding noise along the ship's starboard side. *Titanic*'s bow had turned to port about two points of the compass before impact. Using calculations taken from *Olympic*, it could be determined that *Titanic* could turn that distance in 37 seconds when travelling at 22 knots. It appeared to be a sideswipe, as some ice broke off the berg and landed in the forward Well Deck. The lookouts described the impact as 'a narrow shave'.

The forward end of *Titanic*'s A Deck. The seaman standing watch is Quartermaster Alfred Olliver, who would be the standby quartermaster on the bridge when *Titanic* collided with the iceberg. (Author's collection)

The ringing of the crow's nest bell alerted the men on the bridge. The telephone had been answered by Sixth Officer Moody. It was he who reported the conversation immediately to Murdoch, who instinctively rushed to the telegraph to order the engines 'All stop', 'Full astern'.

Contrary to the narratives of many documentaries and the retelling of the *Titanic* tragedy by countless speakers, *Titanic* never would have been able to stop nor be reversed in thirty-seven seconds. Unlike petrol or oil-powered engines with transmissions, steam-powered triple-expansion engines with the control valves wide open and the ship travelling at some 22–22.5 knots, could not undertake an emergency manoeuvre that fast.

37
Period Ship's Wheel

This period mahogany ship's wheel, 3ft 9in in diameter, was purchased with a brass hub over the shaft opening with a White Star Line stamp on it. Though it is unknown what ship this came from, or why it is stamped with the White Star Line logo, it is of the period, dimensions and style of the three fitted to *Titanic*.

Titanic's main steering wheel was located in the Wheelhouse, and this is where the ship was normally steered from at sea. A secondary wheel was located in the Navigating Bridge, just forward of the Wheelhouse for use in pilotage waters, and a third wheel was located on the Docking Bridge on the Poop Deck for emergency use.

Titanic's wheel acted the same as did the wheel on all British vessels of the era, in that, when steering the ship, the wheel was rotated in the opposite direction to the steering command. For 'starboard the helm', the top of the wheel was turned to port and the ship's head went to port. To 'port the helm', the top of the wheel was turned to starboard.

The history behind this steering command dates back to the era when ships were steered by a tiller, which was moved in the opposite direction of the intended movement. By the end of the First World War, the maritime community had standardised the steering commands to correspond with the direction in which the top of the wheel was turned. Relative to the sequence of events on the night of *Titanic*'s sinking, this command had (and still does) caused endless confusion to mariners and historians alike. When Quartermaster Hichens received the order 'hard a-starboard', he was being given a command to turn the wheel counter-clockwise, thus turning the bow to port.

Quartermaster Hichens later recalled:

At 10 o'clock I went to the wheel. Mr. Murdoch come up to relieve Mr. Lightoller. I had the course given me from the other quartermaster, north 71 west, which I repeated to him, and he went and reported it to the first officer or the second officer in charge, which he repeated back ... All went along very well until 20 minutes to 12, when three gongs came from the look-out, and immediately afterwards a report on the telephone, 'Iceberg right ahead'. The chief officer rushed from the wing to the bridge, or I imagine so ... Certainly I am enclosed in the wheelhouse, and I cannot see, only my compass. He rushed to the engines. I heard the telegraph bell ring; also give the order 'Hard a starboard', with the sixth officer standing by me to see the duty carried out and the quartermaster standing by my

left side. Repeated the order, 'Hard a starboard. The helm is
hard over, sir.'

Down in Boiler No. 6, Head Stoker Frederick Barrett heard the
Boiler Room telegraph bell ring. He saw the red light on the illu-
minated telegraph indicating 'STOP'. He and Second Engineer
Hesketh immediately called out to 'shut the dampers'.

Up on the bridge, Captain Smith came rushing out of his room
and asked Murdoch, 'What have we struck?'

'An iceberg Sir, I hard-a-starboarded and I was going to hard-
a-port around it but she was too close. I could not do any more.
I have closed the watertight doors.'

'The watertight doors are closed? And have you rung the warning bell?'

'Yes, Sir.'

Smith ordered Fourth Officer Boxhall to inspect the forward
area below, and report back to him as quickly as possible. He went
directly to the lowest passenger deck forward, between No. 2 and
3 hatches on G Deck. During Boxhall's return to the bridge, he
inspected all the decks in the vicinity of the impact but saw no
damage. On the bridge, Captain Smith moved the telegraphs to
'Half-speed ahead', which occurred for only a few minutes until
the engines were stopped.

Smith sent for Thomas Andrews, Harland & Wolff's Managing
Director, who was aboard as part of the Guarantee Group, to come
to the bridge. Meanwhile, Fourth Officer Boxhall returned topside
to convey his findings. After his report, Smith ordered Boxhall to
get the ship's carpenter to sound the ship.

Ismay arrived on the bridge at about 11.47 p.m. and was advised
by Andrews that the ship was badly damaged. Ismay returned
below decks, after which Smith and Andrews went on to inspect
the damage themselves. Unknown to the officers at that time,
Titanic had sustained damage to all six watertight compartments
forward of No. 4 Boiler Room. They were open to the sea from
damage about 10ft above the keel for a distance covering 300ft in
the form of intermittent jagged gashes.

There was damage in the forepeak, No. 1 Hold, No. 2 Hold,
No. 3 Hold, No. 6 Boiler Room and No. 5 Boiler Room. Though

The Navigating Bridge of the *Olympic* showing a number of instruments, including the engine and steering order telegraphs, binnacle and one of the ship's wheels. This one was used only when entering or leaving port. (Taken by Francis Browne/author's collection)

No. 5 Boiler Room was damaged at the ship's side, water was pouring in as it would from an ordinary fire hose.

Titanic was damaged beyond the safety limits designed into her hull. Her watertight compartments were not sealed at the top and therefore the water rose in the compartments and poured over the tops of the bulkheads into the next adjacent compartment aft. The water entering these compartments was coming in faster than the pumps could remove it. At some point, *Titanic* would go into negative buoyancy and sink.

Thomas Andrews came on the bridge shortly after midnight. After hearing of the events of the impact, he made calculations based on the amount of water that had entered *Titanic* since the time of collision and found that the ship had but an hour and a half to stay afloat. The pumps were incapable of keeping up with the amount of water entering the vessel and would only buy some extra time, nothing more.

With that said, Smith ordered Chief Officer Wilde to have the sixteen lifeboats and four collapsible boats readied, with the realisation that there was only enough capacity to evacuate half of the passengers aboard. Second Officer Lightoller took command of the port side, while First Officer Murdoch took the starboard, with Fifth Officer Lowe and Sixth Officer Moody assisting where needed.

Titanic lay still on the water, seemingly derelict, the lights of her decks reflecting off the motionless water and quiet. Suddenly, the roar of the steam blowing off from the relief valves down in the Boiler Rooms interrupted the silence. The noise was so loud that it was described as 'twenty locomotives blowing off steam in a low key'. Conversation was nearly impossible, but the sound was soon over, and the silence returned.

Marconi Room Style Gimbal Lamp

Earlier in the voyage, First Class passenger Frank Browne was taking pictures in areas around *Titanic*'s decks and was allowed in the Officers' Quarters Deckhouse. He happened to take an image looking into the door of the Marconi Room with Junior Wireless Operator Harold Bride at the desk. Above Bride's head was a gimbal lamp, attached to the bulkhead, which was very similar to the artefact shown here. Browne disembarked at Queenstown, taking his negatives with him.

The developed image turned out to be a double exposure and was nearly discarded by Browne until he heard that *Titanic* had sunk. Browne had taken the only image of *Titanic*'s Marconi Room. Harold Bride survived on Collapsible B, but Jack Phillips did not.

Titanic's Marconi suite was located centrally on the Boat Deck within the Officers' Quarters Deckhouse. It consisted of three interconnected rooms abreast of each other. On the starboard side were the Marconi operators' quarters. In the middle was the Operator's Room, which contained the main operator's table. This is where the Morse key was located. The port-side compartment was the Silent Room, which was essentially a 'room inside a room', designed to muffle the sound of the rotary spark disc.

Jack Phillips was working the key when Captain Smith ordered a distress signal be sent out. Phillips initially sent out the code 'CQD MGY', the 'CQ' being the proprietary Marconi code for 'all stations' while the 'D' stood for 'urgent'. 'MGY' were *Titanic*'s call letters. All of the shipping lines using the Marconi wireless system knew the proprietary codes.

The first wireless distress message from *Titanic* was sent out at 12.27 a.m., about the same time the order was given to begin loading the boats with women and children. The message was received by the steamships *La Provence*, *Mount Temple* and *Frankfurt*, and the land station at Cape Race. This message, utilising the Marconi proprietary code of 'CQD', was sent with coordinates 41° 44′ N, 50° 24′ W.

The steamer *Frankfurt* was the first to respond. With this, Phillips sent Bride out to inform Captain Smith. Bride found the Captain out on the starboard Boat Deck, superintending the loading of the lifeboats that had been ordered a short time before. The

First Class passenger Francis Browne photographed the only image of *Titanic*'s Marconi Room, with Harold Bride at the desk. (Francis Browne/author's collection)

original 'CQD' coordinates were found to be inaccurate by Smith and his deck officers, so a recalculation was undertaken.

At 12.37 a.m., Phillips sent out a wireless distress message with the corrected coordinates of 41° 46' N, 50° 14' W. These were the coordinates that were picked up by the rescue ship *Carpathia*. A short time later, Captain Smith ordered that the distress signal 'SOS' be used instead of 'CQD', as 'SOS' was known by ships' operators who were using other manufacturers' equipment. 'SOS' was a standard code approved by a committee of the International Wireless Telegraph Convention held in 1908, the letters being chosen only because of the ease of transmission. The letters 'SOS' are represented by an unbroken sequence of three dots / three dashes / three dots, with no spaces between the letters.

Perhaps Smith felt his only hope was a response from the distress signals by a ship whose lights were seen some 6 miles away. Smith directed Fourth Officer Boxhall to fire off socket distress signals, which were much like a modern firework, travelling high into the air and exploding to throw out an array of illuminated stars. Firing the socket signals was an attempt to attract the vessel that was first sighted off *Titanic*'s port bow to the north while crew members were first clearing the boats.

The first socket signal was sent up as Lifeboat No. 3 was being filled with passengers at about 12.27 a.m. With the explosion of the distress rockets fired at short intervals, many passengers started to finally realise the danger they were in, especially in Third Class.

It would be found later that *Titanic*'s socket signals were seen from the bridge of Leyland Line's *Californian*, which was stopped at the eastern edge of the field pack ice to the north of where *Titanic* was. Eight white rockets, in all, were seen by *Californian*. Despite knowing that these were distress signals, the second officer on *Californian*, who was in charge of the deck at the time, failed to grasp the meaning of what was being witnessed.

Corresponding with Fourth Officer Boxhall firing the rockets from *Titanic*'s bridge, communication was also attempted with the use of the Morse signalling lamp. These lamps were located on top of the bridge wings, and it was hoped again to contact the vessel in the distance. Boxhall would later testify:

> *There were a lot of stewards and men standing around the Bridge and around the Boat Deck. Of course, there were quite a lot of them quite interested in this ship, looking from the Bridge, and some said she had shown a light in reply, but I never saw it. I even got the quartermaster who was working around with me – I do not know who he was – to fire off the distress signal, and I got him to also signal with the Morse lamp – that is just a series of dots with short intervals of light – whilst I watched with a pair of glasses to see whether this man did answer, as some people said he had replied. There was no reply.*

39

White Star Line Lifeboat

This is one of the last surviving White Star Line lifeboats. The darkness that surrounds the boat gives a glimpse into what might have been experienced on the morning of 15 April 1912, when passengers looked down onto the boats they were told to enter. In the cold air, away from the warmth of the interior of the ship, one had to decide whether to enter a boat that would be lowered into the darkness or stay on an unsinkable ship.

'How could this have happened?' some thought. The challenge of getting passengers into the boats early in the evacuation of *Titanic* was due to the belief that the ship was unsinkable.

This lifeboat is from White Star Line tender *Nomadic*, which was used at Cherbourg for decades after 1912. She made it through two world wars and saw the White Star Line absorbed by Cunard in 1934, then the eventual full demise of the White Star name with the scrapping of *Britannic III* in 1960.

Nomadic, by then renamed *Ingenieur Minard*, continued to carry passengers to the Cunard liners – including the two great queens: *Elizabeth* and *Mary*. After serving *Queen Elizabeth* in November 1968, *Nomadic* was sent to the breaker's yard. However, she escaped the cutting torches when she was purchased and converted to a floating restaurant on the River Seine, near the Eiffel Tower. After a time, the restaurant failed, and eventually the French Government seized *Nomadic* in lieu of outstanding mooring fees.

Belfast Industrial Heritage Ltd campaigned for nearly five years to bring SS *Nomadic* back to the city of her birth and, following an approach to John White and David Scott-Beddard of White Star Memories, an Internet appeal, 'savenomadic.com', was launched in 2005, bringing the plight of *Nomadic* to thousands of *Titanic* enthusiasts around the world.

Such was the success of the campaign that the Northern Ireland Government approached the savenomadic.com team and liaised

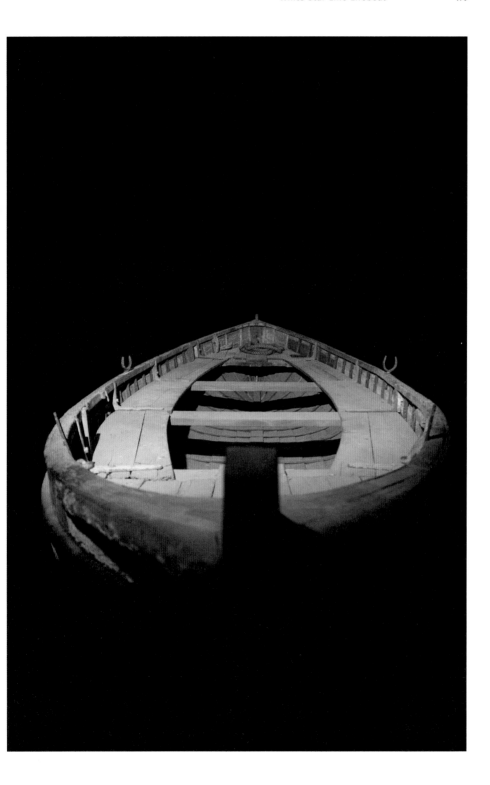

closely with them, leading to the Northern Ireland Department of Social Development (City Centre Regeneration) purchasing the vessel at auction in Paris on 26 January 2006.

Nomadic arrived back in Belfast aboard a floating barge on 15 July that same year and was put on display at a quayside in Belfast for five days. Thousands of visitors flocked to Belfast's Laganside to see her, leading to the savenomadic.com group forming the Nomadic Preservation Society, which attracted almost 1,000 members in its first year!

Three of the original team, David Scott-Beddard, Rupert Keyzar and Mervyn Pritchard, were employed by the new owners to oversee the initial restoration of the vessel and dozens of volunteers worked on the ship, until Harland & Wolff took the project over in 2009. SS *Nomadic* is now on display in the Hamilton Dry Dock, opposite the '*Titanic* Belfast' visitor attraction.

Of the two original 20ft lifeboats installed on *Nomadic*, No. 2 was the only one to survive. Purchased by the *Nomadic* Preservation Society from the Musée Maritime Chantereyne in Cherbourg-Octeville, France, and following restoration, it was leased to White Star Memories for exhibition. It is pictured here as it appeared on display in 2017, on *Queen Mary* in Long Beach, California.

Once the order was given to start loading the lifeboats, the officers in general started from forward to aft. First Officer Murdoch, Third Officer Pitman and Fifth Officer Lowe worked on the forward starboard lifeboats, while Second Officer Lightoller started on the forward port-side boats.

While Fourth Officer Boxhall was sending up distress rockets, Sixth Officer Moody was busy uncovering the lifeboats on the port side aft. In the meantime, Captain Smith and Chief Officer Wilde were busy generally superintending the evacuation.

Despite popular belief, there is substantial evidence that Captain Smith was heavily involved in all aspects of the evacuation and the boat loading and lowering process, and that Chief Officer Wilde was heavily involved in the loading of the boats.

As the evacuation progressed, the officers moved aft to load boats and control the crowds gathering there. The four collapsible boats could not be used until the forward davits were clear of Lifeboats Nos 1 and 2 and were not used until the rest of the lifeboats were away from the ship.

The passengers who were forced to leave their quarters because of flooding in the early stages were the single Third Class men, who were berthed in the areas forward towards the bow in what was termed 'steerage'. These men ascended to the Well Deck, some with their luggage, where a group of approximately fifty to 100 remained for a while. The route from this part of the ship to the central structure of *Titanic* at B Deck was obstructed by an unlocked low gate. Third Class stewards were seen conversing with the men who had gathered at that location, and perhaps they informed the men that only women and children were allowed to go to the boats at that time.

First Class and most Second Class passengers reported no difficulty gaining access to the Boat Deck or to A Deck, where the lifeboats were loaded. Third Class passengers in the aft end of the ship, including both men and women, congregated on the stern Well Deck, up on the Poop Deck, and also in the Third Class General Room under the Poop Deck.

Those who attempted to get to the Boat Deck found themselves stopped by stewards at the top of a set of stairs leading to B Deck. These gates were unlocked, but this seemed to have been unknown at the time. Later, the gates would be opened up, but those ascending the stairs found that many of the lifeboats had already left the ship. However, there were Third Class passengers escorted up through the Second and First Class areas to the lifeboats by Steward John Hart.

There was no organised effort to evacuate Third Class passengers. Third Class passenger Berk Pickard would later testify that many of the stewards and passengers, himself included, did not know the ship was sinking. The stewards tried to keep them quiet, saying that nothing was seriously wrong and reassuring them in general.

At first it was difficult convincing First and Second Class passengers to enter the boats. Lawrence Beesley recalled:

No signs of alarm were exhibited by any one: there was no indication of panic or hysteria; no cries of fear, and no running to and fro to discover what was the matter, why we had been summoned on deck with lifebelts, and what was to be done with us now that we were there.

40

Exterior Bulkhead Light

This exterior bulkhead lamp from *Olympic* is the same as those used on *Titanic*. Lamps such as this example with the protective bars were used in the Well Decks. The design of these lamps was referred to as the 'oyster' type, and they were supplied by William McGeoch & Co. Ltd as the Glasgow agents for N. Burt & Co. The lights were fixed to the deck head or on the sides of the deckhouses and railings.

Unlike Hollywood movie sets depicting the Boat and Weather Decks with added spotlights on the funnels and additional illumination for the purposes of filming, the actual exterior of *Titanic* was not nearly as well lit. These bulkhead lights are some 9¼in diameter and were spaced approximately 20ft apart on the ship.

Their illumination was rated at some 16 candlepower, which is about equal to a 15-watt ceiling fan lightbulb.

Lawrence Beesley wrote how the water 'looked a tremendous way down in the darkness, the sea and the night both seemed very cold and lonely; and here was the ship, so firm and well lighted and warm'. Beesley was obviously referring to the interior of *Titanic* being well lit and warm, not where the lifeboats were being loaded out on the Boat Deck in the below-freezing weather.

On the Promenade Deck, Steward Arthur Lewis saw ladies strolling arm in arm and pleaded with them to get into a lifeboat. 'We're alright, Steward, the ship can't sink,' some would respond. Mr D.H. Bishop stated that there was no danger, and the general feeling was that those who had put off in lifeboats were making fools of themselves and would have the trouble of rowing back to the boat again after a few hours.

Many of the victualling crew members were unaware of the graveness of the situation. With the lack of an internal ship's communication system, all word was mouth to mouth. Cabin stewards were assuring passengers that all was well, while some of their counterparts, unknowingly, were setting up the dining saloons for the next morning's breakfast. Even the gymnasium instructor was still helping passengers on the mechanical exercise equipment.

It was said that last drinks were 'on the house' in the First Class Smoking Room, the same location where Major Archibald Butt and Frank Millet chose to retire. The men sat at a table and played a final hand of cards before going their own way.

The ship's musicians, dressed in their company uniforms, assembled outside the First Class Lounge and were seen playing 'Great Big Beautiful Doll', 'Alexander's Ragtime Band' and other upbeat tunes. Later, they would move to the Boat Deck at the First Class staircase foyer to continue playing as the lifeboats were being loaded.

Bishop further stated:

There was a sense of the whole thing being a dream … that those who walked the decks or tied one another's life jackets on were actors in a scene … that the dream would end soon and we should wake up … Eventually it came to a point where some women were picked up bodily by crewmen and dropped

into the lifeboats. Their husbands hurriedly kissed them good-
bye expecting to follow them in another lifeboat or to rejoin
them in New York.

Benjamin Guggenheim and his manservant, Victor Giglio, removed their life jackets and changed into their elegant suits before returning to deck. Guggenheim said to a steward:

I think there is grave doubt that the men will get off. I am will-
ing to remain and play the man's game if there are not enough
boats for more than the women and children. I won't die here
like a beast. Tell my wife … I played the game out straight and
to the end. No women shall be left aboard this ship because
Ben Guggenheim is a coward.

On the port side, under the supervision of Lightoller, only women and children were generally permitted in the lifeboats, follow-ing an age-old unwritten rule of the sea. On the starboard side, men were allowed to climb in if there were no women in sight. Regardless of which side of the ship, however, very few of the life-boats were loaded anywhere near to their capacity.

At first, the officers refused to fill the boats to the certified capacity because they thought they may buckle under the weight while being lowered down to the water. Passenger Henry Harper remembered stepping into a lifeboat holding his pet Pekinese spaniel, Sun Yat Sen. 'There seemed to be lots of room,' he remarked, 'and nobody made any objection'.

At 12.40 a.m., Lifeboat No. 7, on the starboard side, was launched by Murdoch and Lowe under the charge of Lookout Hogg with twenty-eight people aboard out of a capacity of sixty-five. Included in the passengers on board were Dickinson Bishop and his wife, Helen. A few minutes later, Lifeboat No. 5 was launched with Third Officer Pitman aboard and a passenger count of about thirty-six.

Murdoch and Lowe saw that Lifeboat No. 3 was lowered with around thirty-two on board at 12.55 a.m.

On the port side of the ship, Captain Smith, Chief Officer Wilde and Second Officer Lightoller launched Lifeboat No. 8 at 1.00 a.m.

Able-Bodied Seaman Thomas Jones was in charge, with about twenty-five people aboard.

Passengers Isidor and Ida Straus came near Lifeboat No. 8 as it was being loaded, but Mr Straus declared he would not get in until all women and children had been safely taken off the ship. With that, Mrs Straus refused to leave her husband's side, stating, 'We have been living together for many years, and where you go, I go'. After giving her fur coat to her maid, who had entered the boat, it was said that she and her husband sat down on a bench and watched as the lifeboat was being filled.

Lifeboat No. 1 was launched at about 1.05 a.m. with Lookout George Symons in charge. Having a capacity of forty people, it was lowered with twelve people on board. Lifeboat No. 6, with Quartermaster Robert Hichens in charge, was launched a few minutes later also with twelve people on board.

Although the Captain had ordered some of the lifeboats to 'stand by' in the water with the intent to take passengers off the ship through the gangway doors located along the sides of the hull, this never happened as all the boats rowed away quickly to a distance, for fear that suction would drag them under as the ship sank.

At about 1.20 a.m., Lifeboat No. 16 was lowered under the supervision of Sixth Officer Moody, having ordered Master-at-Arms Henry Bailey to lower himself down via the falls to be in charge of some fifty-two people.

Lifeboat No. 14, launched at about 1.25 a.m., under the supervision at various times of Chief Officer Wilde, Second Officer Lightoller and Fifth Officer Lowe. However, Lowe superintended the final loading and lowering and assumed command of the lifeboat when it reached the water. It is believed No. 14 was lowered with around forty people. Among the passengers was Mr Butler Aspinall, who had assisted in loading a number of boats prior to boarding this one. Aspinall would later testify:

Directly I got to my boat I jumped in, saw the plug in, and saw my dropping ladder was ready to be worked at a moment's notice; and then Mr. Wilde, the Chief Officer, came along and said, 'All right; take the women and children,' and we started taking the women and children. There would be

Captain
Smith and
Chief Purser
Hugh McElroy
photographed
for the last time
at Queenstown.
Above McElroy's
head is a
bulkhead
light with
forward-facing,
light-blocking
shield. These
types of lights
did not have
the cage bars
but were of the
same size and
candlepower
as the artefact
shown.
(Author's
collection)

20 women got into the boat, I should say, when some men tried to rush the boats, foreigners they were, because they could not understand the order which I gave them, and I had to use a bit of persuasion. The only thing I could use was the boat's tiller.

Aspinall prevented five men getting into the boat:

One man jumped in twice and I had to throw him out the third time … when Mr. Lowe came and took charge he asked me how many were in the boat; I told him as far as I could count there were 54 women and four children, one of those children being a baby in arms. It was a very small baby which came under my notice more than anything, because of the way the mother was looking after it, being a very small child.

Aspinall was in the boat with women, children, two firemen and three or four stewards. When Lowe finally came to get in the boat, Aspinall informed him of the trouble he had with the men rushing to get in.

Lowe pulled out his Browning 9mm and fired two shots into the water between the ship and the boat's side. He issued a warning to the remainder of the men who were nearby that if there was any more rushing, he would use it.

A young boy, however, had managed to leap into the boat and crawled under a seat to hide. Charlotte Collyer and other women covered him with their skirts, but Lowe dragged him to his feet and ordered him out, threatening him with his Browning. The boy climbed out of the lifeboat while the women sobbed.

While Lifeboat No. 14 was being lowered into the water, the stern fall twisted up, causing the boat to tilt at a dangerous angle of about 30 degrees with the bow afloat and the stern up in the air. Aspinall, a man with sailing experience, cut part of the fall, which eased it up. Then, by using the releasing gear on board the boat, it came away from the ship without further incident.

Lifeboat No. 12 launched five minutes after No. 14, with Able-Bodied Seaman John Poingdestre in charge and around forty-two people aboard. At about 1.30 a.m., Murdoch ordered the launching of No. 9, with Boatswain's Mate Albert Haines in charge, although multiple survivor accounts indicate the belief that Able-Bodied Seaman George McGough was in charge of this boat, probably due to the fact that he sat at the tiller. It is estimated that about forty people were aboard Lifeboat No. 9. Able-Bodied Seaman Sidney Humphreys was charged with Lifeboat No. 11, which was launched at about 1.35 a.m. with some fifty people aboard.

Approximately five minutes after No. 11, No. 13 was lowered with Head Stoker Barrett in command after the boat hit the water. It had some fifty-five people on board. First Officer Murdoch oversaw the launching of this boat from the Boat Deck, but Sixth Officer Moody assisted at the A Deck level.

Lawrence Beesley had been permitted to climb in after all the women and children in sight had boarded. The descent, he remembered, was a great adventure:

It was exciting to feel the boat sink by jerks, foot by foot, … thrilling to see the black hull of the ship on one side and the sea, seventy feet below, on the other, or to pass down by cabins and saloons, brilliantly lighted.

Twelve-year-old Ruth Becker was also aboard Lifeboat No. 13 and remembered:

> *We could see the water rushing into the ship. Rowing away, looking at the* Titanic, *it was a beautiful sight outlined against the starry sky, every porthole and saloon blazing with light. It was impossible to think anything could be wrong with such an enormous ship, were it not for the tilt downwards toward the bow. Fear was increasing on* Titanic *as her bow section was submerging even deeper into the water.*

At almost the same time that No. 13 was being lowered, Lifeboat No. 15 was launched under the direction of First Officer Murdoch and with assistance from the deck below by Sixth Officer Moody. Fireman Frank Dymond assumed control of the boat after it was on the water.

No. 15 was the most heavily loaded boat when launched. It was stated that the gunwales of the boat were far down in the water. This observation was supported by the account of Bertha Mulvihill, a Third Class passenger rescued in No. 15, who stated that when she leaned against the gunwale, it was so low that her hair dangled in the water. It is believed that No. 15 was loaded with around sixty-eight aboard.

Lifeboat No. 2 was launched at about 1.45 a.m., under the supervision of both Chief Officer Wilde and Captain Smith. Fourth Officer Boxhall was put in charge of the boat, with only seventeen on board. *Titanic's* propellers were observed as out of the water at this time.

Lifeboat No. 10 was launched five minutes later by First Officer Murdoch, with Able-Bodied Seaman Edward Buley in charge. However, once afloat, Buley was transferred to No. 14 by Fifth Officer Lowe, to go back into the wreckage to look for survivors. This was the last of the port-side boats to be lowered, having roughly fifty-seven people aboard. *Titanic* had taken on a 10-degree list to port which caused a gap between Lifeboat No. 10 and the side of the ship of about 2½ft.

Second Officer Lightoller saw to the launching of Lifeboat No. 4 at about 1.50 a.m., with Quartermaster Walter Perkis in charge and approximately thirty aboard. As No. 4 was being readied for lowering, John Jacob Astor handed his pregnant wife Madeleine into the boat after the millionaire was refused permission to join her. Astor remained on the ship helping other women climb aboard, then stood on deck and waved. The boat descended only some 15ft into the water, instead of the usual 70ft distance.

At this point, only the collapsible boats remained on *Titanic*. Up in the Marconi Room, Phillips reported to Bride, who was at the transmitting key, that the forward Well Deck was awash.

Bruce Ismay had been quite active on the starboard side all morning, assisting passengers into boats and generally urging them to get away from the ship. He was standing close to Collapsible C, after it had been secured to the davits from the previously launched Lifeboat No. 1.

First Officer Murdoch was allowing men into the boat as long as there were no women and children waiting to get in. Mrs Emily Goldsmith and her young son Frank entered the boat along with a number of Third Class women and female crew members. Quartermaster Rowe and a number of male crewmen had been ordered into the boat, with Rowe placed in charge.

Seeing there was space available, Ismay and another First Class passenger, William Carter, entered the boat. Along with these passengers were Lee Bing, Ling Hee, Chang Chip and Ah Lam, four Chinese men who were said to be ducking low by the thwarts to go unnoticed. Collapsible C was put off the ship at approximately 2.00 a.m. with approximately forty-three people aboard.

Mr Ismay was later heavily criticised for his escape in the lifeboat because he was one of the owners of the White Star Line. However, he was a passenger, just as anyone else. Ismay's escape created mixed emotions from those who feel he was justified and those who feel he should not have taken the space of any women or children. In any case, Ismay left on Collapsible C, working at an oar, with his back to the ship so as to avoid having to watch the end.

Collapsible D was launched at about 2.05 a.m., as the Fo'c'sle head was seen going under, supervised by Chief Officer Wilde and Second Officer Lightoller. To hold back the rushing people, Lightoller ordered the crew to form a circle around Collapsible D to ensure only women and children boarded the boat.

A Frenchman who had listed himself as 'M. Hoffman' passed his two little boys, Michel and Edmond, off to a crewman in the boat. Quartermaster Arthur Bright was put in command of about twenty people, but three male passengers climbed aboard while the boat was still hanging from the falls before it landed in the water.

At this late stage, Captain Smith relieved the wireless operators and other crew members of their duties and advised them to look to their own safety. Marconi Operator Phillips stayed at his post, as did thirty-four engineers, plumbers, electricians and Boiler Room crew members. On deck, a group of men struggled to launch Collapsible B, while in Third Class, steerage passenger August Wennerstrom recalled, 'Hundreds were in a circle with a preacher in the middle, praying and crying'. Others fell or jumped from the ship.

At 2.10 a.m., *Titanic*'s bow lunged deeper under the surface, causing the water to rush over the deck. One lifeboat passenger recalled:

> There was a sudden rush of passengers on all decks toward the stern. It was like a wave. We could see the great black mass of people in the steerage sweeping to the rear part of the boat and breaking through the upper decks.

Collapsibles A and B were attached to the roof of the Officers' Quarters Deckhouse and required the use of a special tackle attached to an eye located within the funnel shrouds. These falls were stowed forward in the bow, but by the time Murdoch and Moody were ready to launch Collapsible A, the storeroom was well under water.

With that said, Collapsible A was washed off the Boat Deck around 2.15 a.m. Most of the occupants of Collapsible A climbed in from the water. Over the course of the morning of the 15th, many died and fell back into the sea. The number left alive when picked up by Collapsible D was probably twelve or thirteen, including just one woman.

41

Bridge Megaphone from *Olympic*

This megaphone from the *Olympic* is identical to that from *Titanic* that was raised from the wreck site. The megaphone was used for voice commands from the bridge, such as when Captain Smith was ordering the lifeboats to return to the ship to pick up passengers from gangways or other means – an order none of them followed.

One of the men standing on Collapsible B was Butler Aspinall, who was one of the last people to see Captain Smith alive. He stated in his testimony that when he was assisting with unsecuring a collapsible boat:

> *The Captain came past us while we were trying to get this boat away with a megaphone in his hand, and he spoke to us … He said, 'Well, boys, do your best for the women and children, and look out for yourselves'. He then walked to the bridge.*

Collapsible B was washed off the Boat Deck upside down at about 2.15 a.m. Second Officer Lightoller and a number of others pushed the boat from the roof of the Officers' Deckhouse, where it landed upside down on the Boat Deck below. Soon thereafter, just as the forward section of the Boat Deck submerged under water, with water coming over the bridge railing, the boat was washed away.

Lightoller climbed aboard the collapsible and took command after experiencing near death having been sucked onto the grate of the forward ventilation duct. A blast of hot water pushed him off. Later in the morning, approximately twenty-eight occupants were found standing in water up to their knees on the swamped Collapsible B.

In a matter of minutes after 'the ship left' Lightoller, the stern was seen well out of the water as the bow pitched down suddenly. Passenger Jack Thayer had dived into the water and clung to the overturned Collapsible B. Thayer watched as, he later stated:

> *… groups of the almost fifteen hundred people still aboard, clinging in clusters or bunches, like swarming bees; only to fall in masses, pairs or singly, as the great after part of the ship, two hundred and fifty feet of it, rose into the sky …*

42

Wallace Hartley's Sheet Music

Wallace Hartley's body was recovered by the *Mackay-Bennett* almost two weeks after the sinking. Several press reports confirmed that Wallace was found 'fully dressed with his music case strapped to his body'. Inside that case was his violin (a gift from his fiancée, Maria Robinson) and a leather valise containing his sheet music. One of his favourite compositions was the 'Starland Intermezzo' by Will G. Markwith and this was one of the pieces inside his valise.

The ship's musicians had continued to play as the angle of *Titanic*'s decks became more and more extreme. Bandleader Hartley continued to conduct his musicians as the ship was sinking. He had released them from duty sometime prior, but all chose to remain together and continue to play. At the end they were heard playing a final, solemn tune. Some said the name of the song was 'Autumn', others remembered the hymn 'Nearer my God to Thee'.

All the lights went out when the steam pipes feeding the generators ruptured. *Titanic* appeared to split in two abaft the aft expansion joint, with the stern righting itself without the bow. Nearly 1,500 lives remained, as the stern section went down at 2.20 a.m. – 817 passengers and 679 crew, 1,496 people in all. Among those lost were Chief Joseph Bell and his engineering staff of over thirty men who stayed at their posts the whole time.

During the early morning hours, Lifeboats Nos 4, 10, 12, 14 and Collapsible D tied up together and a number of transfers of passengers were made between them. No. 14 was lowered with around forty occupants, but Lowe transferred almost all of these to other lifeboats before he took a very empty lifeboat back into the debris to look for survivors.

Lowe was left with six volunteers to accompany him in No. 14, the only boat to return for any survivors. When No. 14 came back to the wreckage, various cries were heard and Lowe endeavoured to get to them. He was successful in picking up one person who was floating in the water. Lowe stated:

> When we got him into the boat – after great difficulty, he being such a heavy man – he expired shortly afterwards. Going farther into the wreckage we came across a steward or one of the crew, and we got him into the boat, and he was very cold and his hands were kind of stiff, but we got him in and he recovered by the time we got back to the Carpathia.

The last survivor to be picked up in the water was a Chinese man found floating on a piece of panelling from the First Class Lounge. Fang Lang became one of the most remarkable survivors. Unable to reach a lifeboat, he ended up in the ocean, floating on wreckage. After enduring sub-zero temperatures, he was pulled, half-frozen but alive, from the wreckage. Fang Lang was revived by the women in the boat, who rubbed his hands, arms and legs to warm his skin. In a matter of time, Lang was able to assist with rowing the boat.

The Rescue

The Cunard liner *Carpathia* was sailing from New York, having left on 11 April, bound for Gibraltar and other Mediterranean ports. Approximately 760 passengers were on board, mostly in Third Class. Having accommodations for some 2,550 passengers, the ship was mostly vacant. *Carpathia* was commanded by Captain Arthur Rostron, an Extra Master with twenty-seven years of seagoing experience – a seasoned captain.

Carpathia's wireless equipment was an older 1½ kW installation, which had a range, in good conditions, of about 250 miles. The wireless room was housed in a small structure above the Second Class Smoking Room with a single operator, Harold Cottam, who was berthed next to the equipment. Cottam worked generally from morning to midnight.

It was a bit after midnight when Cottam prepared to retire. Normally, he would have been in bed but on this night, he was waiting for a response from an earlier communication with the Allen liner *Parisian*. He was in the process of undressing while keeping his headset on. He removed his jacket and bent over to unlace his boots.

After hearing nothing from *Parisian*, Cottam quickly dialled in the frequency to the powerful Cape Cod land station with the intention of listening for messages of general interest. What he heard were messages intended for *Titanic* with no response.

After jotting down the Cape Cod messages to forward them on to *Titanic* in the morning, he dialled back to the frequency used by the ships at sea. Half an hour after his usual bedtime and fighting a knot in his shoelace, Cottam decided to call *Titanic* to inform them of the messages coming in from Cape Cod:

```
MPA (Carpathia): I say, old man, do you know
there is a batch of messages coming through
for you from MCC (Cape Cod)?

MGY (Titanic): (Breaking in): Come at once.
We have struck an iceberg. It's CQD, old man.
Position 41 46' N, 50 14' W

MPA: Shall I tell my captain? Do you require
assistance?

MGY: Yes. Come quick.
```

Cottam noted the time was 10.35 p.m. New York time and hurried to the bridge, where he reported *Titanic*'s signal to First Officer Horace Dean. Dean and Cottam quickly went to Captain Rostron's cabin, where they found him in his bunk, although awake, and gave him the news. Rostron roughly estimated the direction of *Titanic* and ordered Dean to steer north-west at top speed until he could provide more accurate coordinates.

Satisfied the emergency was real, Rostron went to his chartroom to calculate his location using dead reckoning. *Carpathia*'s position was 41° 10' N, 49° 12' W, about 58 miles from the CQD. Rostron ordered Dean to steer the new course.

Carrying on like the experienced Captain he was, he mustered his crew heads and ordered his Chief Engineer to call out an extra watch of firemen and trimmers and drive *Carpathia* as hard as possible. The lookout was increased, with two men being placed in the ship's bow and one in the crow's nest. Three officers and a quartermaster kept watch from *Carpathia*'s bridge.

Perhaps knowing that he would be questioned as to his actions, Rostron notated his orders while en route to *Titanic*:

English doctor, with assistants, to remain in first-class dining room; Italian doctor, with assistants, to remain in second-class dining room; Hungarian doctor, with assistants, to remain in third-class dining room; Each doctor to have supplies of restoratives, stimulants, and everything to hand for immediate needs of probable wounded or sick; Purser, with Assistant Purser and Chief Steward, to receive the passengers, etc., at different gangways, controlling our own stewards in assisting Titanic passengers to the dining rooms, etc.; also to get Christian and surnames of all survivors as soon as possible to send by wireless; Inspector, steerage stewards, and master-at-arms to control our own steerage passengers and keep them out of the third-class dining hall, and also to keep them out of the way and off the deck to prevent confusion; Chief Steward to see that all hands would be called and to have coffee, etc., ready to serve out to all our crew – have coffee, tea, soup, etc., in each saloon, blankets in saloons, at the gangways, and some for the boats; see all rescued cared for and immediate wants attended to; My cabin and all officials' cabins to be given up. Smoke rooms, library, etc., dining rooms, to be utilized to accommodate the survivors; All spare berths in steerage to be utilized for Titanic's passengers, and get all our own steerage passengers grouped together; Stewards to be placed in each alleyway to reassure our own passengers, should they inquire about noise in getting our boats out, etc., or the working of engines. To all I strictly enjoined the necessity for order, discipline and quietness and to avoid all confusion; Chief and first officers: All the hands to be called; get coffee, etc. Prepare and swing out all boats. All gangway doors to be opened; Electric clusters in each gangway and over side; A block with line rove hooked in each gangway; A chair sling at each gangway, for getting up sick or wounded; Boatswains' chairs. Pilot ladders and canvas ash bags to be at each gangway, the canvas ash bags for children; Cargo falls with both ends clear; bowlines in the ends, and bights secured along ship's sides, for boat ropes or to help the people up; Heaving lines distributed along the ship's side, and gaskets handy near gangways for lashing people in chairs, etc; Forward derricks, topped and rigged, and steam on winches; also told off officers for different stations and for certain eventualities; Ordered company's rockets to be fired at 2.45 a.m. and every quarter of an hour after to reassure Titanic.

While these orders were being carried out, Harold Cottam tended rigorously to his wireless set, being assisted by one of the stewards, who delivered each message from *Titanic* to the bridge for Captain Rostron.

At 12.50 a.m., to *Olympic:*

```
I require immediate assistance.
```

At 1.10 a.m., to *Olympic*:

```
We are in collision with berg. Sinking head
down. Come as soon as possible. Get your
boats ready.
```

At 1.25 a.m.:

```
We are putting the women off in small boats.
```

1.35 a.m.:

```
Engine room getting flooded.
```

1.45 a.m.:

```
Engine room full up to the boilers.
```

This was the last *Titanic* signal Cottam heard directly. During this time, Rostron was issuing his specific orders in anticipation of reaching *Titanic*'s location. At 2.30 a.m., Chief Officer Thomas Hankinson reported everything was ready.

Carpathia's nominal top speed was 14½ knots, but the Engine Room crew were able to get the speed up to 17½ knots, which goes to demonstrate the amount of sweat put in by the stokers in feeding the boilers constantly and aggressively. Surely the increased speed amplified any sort of vibration *Carpathia* had, to the point that the passengers could feel that something was awry. The actions of the stewards, loss of heat in the compartments due to the diversion of steam and the general noise of movement out in the alleyways brought the cabin passengers out to ask questions.

Carpathia hurried at first through open water, but later met isolated icebergs. Changes of course were made as required. Captain Rostron would later describe the situation:

> More and more now we were all keyed up. Icebergs loomed up and fell astern; we never slackened, though sometimes we altered course suddenly to avoid them. It was an anxious time with the Titanic's fateful experience very close in our minds. There were seven hundred souls on Carpathia; these lives, as well as all the survivors of Titanic herself, depended on a sudden turn of the wheel.

Shortly after 2.30 a.m., the first of a number of green flares, fired periodically by Fourth Officer Joseph Boxhall in Lifeboat No. 2, was sighted off in the distance.

At 3.00 a.m., Rostron ordered rockets fired at fifteen-minute intervals, as well as Carpathia's company signals to alert anyone at Titanic's location that help was soon to arrive. At 3.35 a.m., Carpathia was near to the position of Titanic, if she was still afloat, but all that could be seen was the vast emptiness of the ocean.

Approaching 4 a.m., a steady green light from a lifeboat was finally sighted about 300 yards directly ahead. Rostron ordered 'ahead slow' and sounded his whistles to advise that they had arrived. Having to avoid a small iceberg, Carpathia stopped her engines and took the incoming lifeboats off her starboard side.

By 4.10 a.m., Fourth Officer Boxhall's boat was alongside Carpathia with only twenty-five female passengers in a boat intended for forty. The women were taken on board, using a combination of rope ladders, slings and bags. Fourth Officer Boxhall, who reported directly to the bridge, informed Captain Rostron that Titanic had sunk, leaving her lifeboats in the general area.

With lookouts posted at the forepeak and in the crow's nest on the forward mast, Carpathia dodged through the ice, pausing to take aboard survivors, then moving slowly ahead to the next lifeboat. One after another, the boats arrived – all that remained of the

Titanic which, not five hours earlier, had been in the midst of her maiden voyage.

At 6.15 a.m., Collapsible C with Bruce Ismay aboard came beside. At 7.00 a.m., Lifeboat No. 14 with Collapsible D in tow came alongside. During the night, Fifth Officer Lowe had transferred twelve men and one woman from a half-swamped Collapsible A to D, leaving three bodies aboard Collapsible A, which was set adrift with the plugs removed (the crew were unaware that the collapsible boats would be swamped with the plugs removed, but they would not sink).

43

Photo of Lifeboat No. 14 and Collapsible D Taken from *Carpathia*

This image of Lifeboat No. 14 with Collapsible D in tow has been reproduced many times over the decades. However, this is the original.

Married in Kentucky on 8 April 1912, James and Mabel Fenwick travelled to New York and sailed three days later as First Class passengers on *Carpathia*, heading for Gibraltar to start their month-long honeymoon. With her Kodak camera, Mabel captured photographs of fellow passengers, *Carpathia*'s Captain Rostron and his fellow officers, along with some of the most dramatic images of *Titanic*'s survivors during the rescue and aboard *Carpathia*.

Fifth Officer Lowe, who was in charge of Lifeboat No. 14, raised the mast and sail in the morning. Lowe had experience in sailing and was the only officer to use his boat's equipment. When approaching *Carpathia*, he lowered the sail to better control the approach to the side of the ship.

Lifeboat Nos 9 and 4 came alongside and, by 8.00 a.m., Lifeboat No. 6 had arrived. Collapsible B was scuttled by the weight, but still afloat, with the water up to the survivors' knees. The men aboard were leaning in unison, at Second Officer Lightoller's command, to the left, then to the right, then back to the left to maintain a knife's-edge balance.

Lightoller, afraid *Carpathia* might not see the boat, blew on his whistle to draw attention. *Carpathia* approached Collapsible B slowly as the waves were starting to kick up. Finally, men were taken aboard, including one who had perished during the night. Lightoller was the last man up the ladder and the final *Titanic* survivor to go aboard.

Of *Titanic*'s 2,208 crew and passengers, there were but 712 living survivors aboard *Carpathia*; 1,496 were lost.

There was silence as the survivors came aboard. Many of the women believed their husbands had been saved by other ships or were taken aboard off another lifeboat. Certainly, the shock of the circumstance took a while to set in before the crying and sobbing began.

As the survivors were cared for and taken to their quarters, Bruce Ismay was escorted to Dr Frank McGee's cabin on the Saloon Deck. The doctor ordered that he be treated in seclusion. Madeleine Force Astor was taken to the infirmary by Gottlieb Rencher, *Carpathia*'s senior hospital attendant.

Shortly after reporting to Dr McGee's quarters, Bruce Ismay was visited by Captain Rostron, who suggested that Ismay notify White Star's New York office about the disaster. Ismay wrote a statement to be transmitted to Philip Franklin, Vice President in the United States for the International Mercantile Marine Co., the parent company of the White Star Line.

The note was taken by Rostron to the radio room for transmission. However, it did not reach the White Star Line's New York offices until after 5.00 p.m. on Wednesday, 17 April. *Carpathia*'s wireless could not send and receive direct ship-to-shore messages, clearly being out of range of New York.

Carpathia had finished picking up survivors by 8.30 a.m. About that time, *Californian* arrived on the scene and began an unsuccessful search for survivors. Having limited room aboard his top decks, Rostron was only able to bring aboard thirteen of the lifeboats, including the two emergency cutters. Lifeboats Nos 4, 14 and 15 and Collapsibles B, C and D were cast adrift, some with the bodies of those who had succumbed to exposure. Collapsible A had been set adrift earlier by Fifth Officer Lowe.

Captain Rostron ordered *Carpathia*'s house flag lowered to half-mast and arranged to have a service in the First Class Saloon conducted as the ship passed over the spot where *Titanic* sank, as near as could be calculated – a service, he said, of respect to those who were lost and gratitude for those who had been saved.

At 8.50 a.m., Rostron ordered *Carpathia* to head west to avoid ice but soon ran into a massive ice field, which required her to sail around for some 56 miles.

After the rescue, some of the survivors aboard *Carpathia* died from shock and exposure: First Class passenger William F. Hoyt, Bedroom Steward Sidney C. Siebert and Able Seaman William Lyons. A Third Class passenger, Abraham Harmer (aka David Livshin), had been taken aboard dead from Collapsible A.

Episcopalian minister the Reverend Father Roger Anderson conducted a memorial service in *Carpathia*'s First Class Lounge at 4.00 p.m. as requested by Captain Rostron. While the reverend recited the benediction, members of *Carpathia*'s crew committed the dead to the sea.

Rostron had to decide where to take the survivors from there. Perhaps the Azores, which was close to his initial destination at Gibraltar, or Halifax, which was close but with the course likely cluttered with ice. The survivors would then have to travel by train to New York. Ultimately, Rostron decided that the best plan was to steam back to New York, which offered the facilities needed to care for the survivors.

In 1913, Captain Rostron wrote an article about the rescue of *Titanic*'s survivors by *Carpathia* for *Scribner's Magazine*. In it, he wrote:

At eight o'clock we also saw a steamer coming toward us out of the ice-field. This ice-field stretched as far as the eye could see from northwest to southeast, and we soon found her to be the Californian. We signalled her and told news of trouble, and asked her to search around, as we were returning to New York. It was now blowing a moderate breeze and the sea was getting up. About eight-twenty or so all the people were aboard, and by eight-forty five all the boats we could take, and then we proceeded to New York. I had decided to return to New York, as I considered New York the only port possible under the circumstances. We soon found our passage blocked by a tremendous ice-field. Of course we had seen this ice-field before, but did not know how compact it was, nor the extent of it. In the field were many bergs from one hundred to one hundred and fifty feet high, and the general mass of ice perhaps six to twelve feet high. We sailed round this ice-pack for nearly four hours – quite fifty-six miles – before we could set our course for New York. We also passed several large bergs clear of the pack.

A roll of survivors was compiled. *Carpathia*'s Chief Purser Ernest G.F. Brown and Second Purser Percy B. Barnett undertook the duties and checked the list of surviving passengers. *Titanic*'s Second Officer Lightoller prepared the list of deck and engine department survivors, while Chief Second Class Steward John Hardy compiled those from the victualling department.

The lists were taken to Harold Cottam, who had been awake for over twenty-four hours at this point. When the survivor lists arrived, Cottam was overwhelmed. He began sending names to *Olympic*, which relayed them to Cape Race. Cottam nearly succumbed to his fatigue, until *Titanic*'s own Junior Wireless Operator Harold Bride came to assist. Bride had been in *Carpathia*'s hospital suffering from severe frostbitten feet but was carried to the Marconi Shack at the request of Rostron and Cottam. The two men ignored all requests from the press and private inquiries, having centred their attention only on survivors' names.

Rostron ordered a news blackout, as there were two newspaper reporters on board as travelling passengers. He forbade interviewing survivors by either of these men, but interviews were taken nonetheless. Also complicating matters was the fact that the wireless transmissions, as far back as the initial calls for CQD on 15 April, were heard and monitored by oceangoing vessels and land stations – not to mention hobbyist wireless operators who monitored navigational traffic. These people leaked stories to the press – and the press in 1912 was just as bad, if not worse than the press of modern times – and each attempted to 'out-scoop' the other, even if it meant bad information and artistic journalism.

The tragedy gripped the world's attention. During Monday and Tuesday, newspaper special editions followed, one after another, each revealing additional details of the accident and the people aboard. Early editions reported on known facts, few as they were: the names of the millionaires and the famous who were known to be aboard. Generalities about *Titanic*'s cost and luxuries intertwined with accounts of other historic shipwrecks – false and invented news stories abounded.

The White Star offices on both sides of the Atlantic were besieged by people wanting to get news of the fate of loved ones or other facts. In the New York offices at 9 Broadway, company officials, aware only that the ship was in distress with no confirmation, made an effort to pacify the crowds.

In the meantime, some of the railroad companies planned special passenger trains to travel to Halifax, where it was assumed the survivors would be landed.

44

Dickinson Letter, Written Aboard *Carpathia*

Helen Bishop penned this letter while aboard *Carpathia*. She and her husband, Dickinson, survived *Titanic* in Lifeboat No. 7. The letter is signed only 'Dickinson'. Though written by Helen, it was not uncommon at the time for the wife to sign herself off under her husband's name.

Delayed by fog and rainy weather, *Carpathia* was expected to dock at Cunard's Pier 54 around 9.00 p.m. on 18 April. The sense of shock and loss prevailed as New York prepared to receive survivors.

Without doubt, depression and sorrow enveloped all aboard, as the vessel, shrouded in fog, cut through the water at a reduced speed on Wednesday morning, 17 April. Driving rain kept most of the passengers in their cabins and quarters.

Ismay's initial message, having been held until within wireless range, was finally sent to Vice President Philip Franklin at the White Star Line's New York office:

```
Deeply regret advise you Titanic sank this
morning fifteenth after collision iceberg
resulting serious loss life further particu-
lars later. Bruce Ismay.
```

Ismay would continue to send a number of messages to Franklin while still aboard *Carpathia*. It is obvious that he knew what was coming when they reached land and realised there would be an investigation.

He intended to get his crew back to England as soon as possible. A wireless message exchange would ensue between the two men, where Ismay wanted *Cedric* held to bring the crew back to

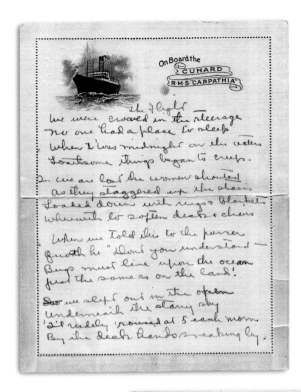

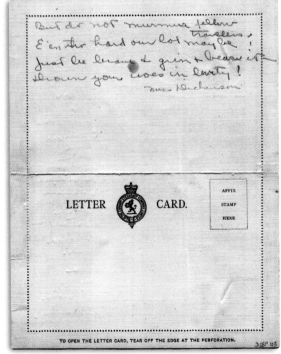

England, but it was the Red Star liner *Lapland*, also owned by
IMM, that would be held for the transport.

As the public anxiously awaited news, one wireless bulletin followed another, but the final confirmation came with the signature
of Bruce Ismay – *Titanic* had indeed foundered, with the loss of
a large number of lives. By 17 April, most survivors' names were
known, having been received from *Carpathia*, relayed first to
Olympic and then by the US Navy Scout Cruiser *Chester* to land-
based telegraphists, who then released the news to the public. At
the New York Maritime Exchange's request, the flags of all shipping in New York Harbor were put to half-mast on Wednesday in
honour of *Titanic*'s dead.

General Nelson H. Henry, Surveyor of the Port, issued orders
that only the closest relatives – father, husband or son, mother,
wife or daughter – would be admitted to the pier upon the arrival
of *Carpathia*, and not more than two would be allowed for each
expected survivor. He had forty inspectors on his staff, and each
request for a pier pass was verified carefully.

The United States Secretary of the Treasury, in a telegram to
New York Surveyor of Customs William Loeb, suspended all of
the usual customs regulations involved in landing survivors and
examining their luggage. Federal immigration officers waived the
usual examination of steerage passengers in an effort to keep the
media away and to assist in relieving some of the trauma already
heaped upon the survivors.

The world anxiously awaited *Carpathia*'s docking at New York
on the evening of Thursday, 18 April.

At 6.00 p.m., *Carpathia* passed the Ambrose Lightship that
marked the entrance to New York, passing a flotilla of small
boats filled with reporters eager for stories from the survivors
who, at this point, were crowding the rails. *Carpathia* slowed
only long enough to take on board the port physician from the
quarantine boat.

Moving through heavy rain and strong winds, *Carpathia*
steamed past the Battery at the southern tip of Manhattan and
proceeded slowly up the Hudson River. She passed her own dock
at 14th Street and came to a stop at the White Star Docks, Piers
58 and 59. Here, she lowered *Titanic*'s remaining lifeboats, which

Carpathia arriving in New York. (Author's collection)

were picked up by the tug *Champion* and towed to the berth between the two piers.

Carpathia moved to her own pier, No. 54, and lowered her gangways at 9.30 p.m. Shortly thereafter, the 318 First and Second Class passengers disembarked, where they were greeted by friends and family who had obtained special passes. Third Class passengers would have to wait until 11.00 p.m. to disembark and most were met by representatives from various relief agencies. Shortly after the Third Class disembarked, the 214 surviving crew walked down the aft gangway, crossed over the pier and immediately boarded the Red Star liner *Lapland*, which was waiting to transport them back to England.

By midnight, Pier 54 stood deserted, except for the guards. Nearly all the survivors had been taken to hotels or shelters.

★

Recovery

Immediately following *Titanic*'s loss, the White Star Line asked its agents in Halifax, Nova Scotia (the nearest major port to the sinking site), to oversee the recovery of victims of the disaster. Passing vessels had reported hundreds of bodies, floating by their white life jackets, generally north-eastward in the Gulf Stream. Warnings to avoid the area were sent by wireless from one vessel to another.

Recovery efforts had begun with *Carpathia*'s arrival on 15 April. Two days later, the first of four vessels chartered by White Star for the grim task arrived on the scene.

The Commercial Cable Company's *Mackay-Bennett*, a cable-laying ship from Halifax, retrieved some 306 bodies and established a procedure that all subsequent searchers would follow. Each victim was assigned a numbered page in a ledger book and a piece of canvas stencilled with the corresponding number was attached to the body. On the ledger page, a full description was written, including hair colour, height, weight, age, scars or birthmarks and a full inventory of the deceased's pockets. Addresses on letters, names on paperwork and ticket numbers were all recorded to assist in identification. Personal property was placed in canvas bags also bearing the victim's number.

Of the 306 bodies found by *Mackay-Bennett*, 116 were too badly decomposed to be brought to port and were buried at sea. The cable ship returned to Halifax on Tuesday, 30 April, with 190 victims aboard, some in caskets, others wrapped in canvas and placed in the ship's ice-filled cable tanks. Once ashore, some victims were photographed, and these photographs were sent to White Star offices that had sold tickets for *Titanic*, in the hope that someone would recognise them.

The second vessel, the Anglo-American Telegraph Company's cable ship *Minia*, arrived at the site on 26 April and returned on 6 May after finding seventeen bodies. The Canadian Government ship *Montmagny* left Sorel, Quebec, on 3 May and returned to Louisbourg, Nova Scotia, on 13 May, having recovered four victims.

White Star's own *Oceanic* came across swamped Collapsible A on 13 May and its three dead occupants were buried at sea.

The final chartered vessel, Bowring Brothers' *Algerine*, left St John's, Newfoundland, on 15 May and recovered a single body, that of Steward James McGrady. By now, sealife and ocean currents made further recoveries doubtful. Of the 336 recovered, 127 were buried at sea, 59 were claimed by loved ones, and the remaining 150 were interred at Halifax's Fairview, Mt Olivet and Baron de Hirsch cemeteries.

Titanic's remaining lifeboats secured at White Star's Berth 54 in New York. Many of the lifeboat names and capacity plates had already been stolen by souvenir collectors or taken as mementos for survivors, before White Star could engage men to guard the boats to prevent looting. (Author's collection)

★

Aftermath

The days following the tragedy were filled with memorial meetings and church services. At noon on Friday, 19 April, a memorial service at St Paul's Cathedral in London drew an overflowing crowd including representatives from the big shipping lines and Alexander Carlisle, former principal architect of Harland & Wolff and designer of the *Olympic*-class ships, who fainted during the service.

Fundraising events to assist *Titanic* survivors were held at Covent Garden and the Royal Albert Hall in London and at the Century Theatre in New York. Every palace or hippodrome in England and America gave benefit performances featuring local talent or, in some instances, the most famous actors, singers, entertainers and orchestras of the day. Thousands of dollars and pounds sterling poured into the relief funds of the American Red Cross, the Salvation Army and Britain's Mansion House.

In Belfast, all of the churches and social groups undertook some form of gathering or service. Many had lost family or friends and, to add to the grief, the pride of Queen's Island was gone. The shipbuilding works of Harland & Wolff were closed on Saturday, 20 April, as well as on Sunday the 21st, which was the general day of mourning for Belfast. Thousands of people attended their local churches as well as a memorial service held in the large hall of the YMCA.

On 22 April 1912, a public meeting at Belfast City Hall opened the Belfast Relief Fund for relatives of those lost on *Titanic*. Donations came in from many people and places, including Lord and Lady Pirrie and Harland & Wolff. When the fund finally closed on 17 May 1912, the donations had reached £2,896.

A *Titanic* Relief Fund was established by the Lord Mayor of London, who invited subscriptions from the public to aid dependent relatives of passengers and crew lost in the sinking. A sum exceeding £413,121 (approximately $2,065,600 at the 1912 exchange rate of £1 to $5) was amassed for distribution to victims' dependants. Lump-sum payments were made to the government officials of those countries where 'foreign cases' resided and the balance was invested by the Mansion House Trustees, the then Lord Mayor, Sir Thomas Boor Crosby and the Public Trustee Mr C.J. Stewart, to create income for the continued support of victims' dependants in Great Britain.

Local area committees, regulated by the Mansion House Committee, were eventually established in cities from where there had been a significant number of victims, such as London, Liverpool, Belfast, Exeter and, of course, Southampton. Of the 673 *Titanic* crew members who were killed, 535 had lived in Southampton, making the city 'the centre of suffering relatives'.

When a relatively complete death toll became known, it was calculated that the *Titanic* Relief Fund would be required to assist 239 widows, 533 children under 16, 42 children over 16 and 213 other dependants, such as parents and siblings who had lived, entirely or partially, on the wages of the deceased.

Initially, Mayor of Southampton Henry Bowyer presided almost single-handedly over the receipt of donations and the payment of relief to local families. However, questions were raised about public accountability for their actions. A local area committee was set up in Southampton towards the end of 1912, but the mayor brushed off calls for wide representation among its members.

As can be imagined, a logistical mess was created in which no one was pleased with the methods of distribution of the monies, but a schedule was created and the fund lasted until 1959, when it was turned into annuities for the sixty-four remaining dependants. The balance of the general fund was transferred to the Shipwrecked Fishermen & Mariners' Royal Benevolent Society. The annuities were administered by the Public Trustee under the direction of the Mansion House Council & Executive Committee.

★

45

Spicer-Simson Medallion Commemorating Captain Rostron of *Carpathia*

This bronze medal is believed to have been commissioned personally by *Titanic* survivor Margaret Brown. Created by Theodore Spicer-Simson, it is not known how many of these medallions were struck. They were said to have been given to Rostron and his crew personally, without the usual fanfare, by

Brown herself. Very little is known about these pieces, but they are extremely rare.*

On the arrival of *Carpathia* in New York on 29 May 1912 from Naples, she was boarded by a committee of *Titanic* survivors headed by Frederic K. Seward. A silver loving cup and gold medal were presented to Captain Rostron by Margaret Brown, after which the crew was assembled in the dining room. All crew members who were present on that day were awarded either a gold, silver or bronze medal produced by Dieges & Clust of New York. The medals bore, in bas-relief, an image of *Carpathia* going at full speed to the rescue of *Titanic*'s victims, while the reverse side bore the following: 'Presented to the Captain and crew of the R.M.S. 'Carpathia' in recognition of their gallant and heroic services, from the survivors of the S.S. 'Titanic', April 15, 1912'.

Chairman Seward spoke to the crew, saying, in part:

The eyes of the world are upon you and were upon you when you came to us on the open ocean, when we saw the Carpathia *coming to us out of the dawn. To all of you we wish to give our heartfelt thanks. For your hospitality, devotion, unselfishness and for all that was done for us we never can be adequately grateful, and as a slight token of that appreciation we wish you to accept the medals that we have had struck for every man and woman of this ship.*

Rostron was honoured with the Congressional Gold Medal, the Thanks of Congress, the American Cross of Honor, and medals from the Liverpool and New York Shipwreck Societies. Rostron would eventually rise to the position of Commodore of the Cunard Line and serve as a British Naval officer during the First World War.

---

* Research undertaken for this writing indicates that Rostron would have scheduled a private sitting with Spicer-Simson, probably in his New York studio, to create the profile sculpt of his piece. Furthermore, the US copyright filed by Spicer-Simson was registered on 6 May 1913: G 43908.

On 29 May 1912, *Carpathia* returned to New York from Naples, her first journey since the dramatic rescue. Once the passengers had left the ship with their baggage, Captain Rostron issued orders for all hands to muster in the First Class Dining Saloon. The 250 members of the crew who were present during the rescue lined up in the saloon in two long lines. As spokesman of the Survivor's Committee, Margaret Brown presented a silver loving cup to Captain Rostron, and a gold, silver or bronze medal to each *Carpathia* crew member. (Author's collection)

★

Limitation of Liability

United States Hearing and Report into the Loss of the Steamship Titanic

The American politicians were already set to place blame and liability, even before *Carpathia* docked. A United States senator from Michigan, William Alden Smith, had put the wheels in motion to form a subcommittee to investigate the incident. Smith was no friend of J.P. Morgan, whose International Mercantile Marine Co. was the ultimate owner of the White Star Line. This gave Smith the impetus to go after Morgan with full force. Smith was not about to allow Ismay or the crew of *Titanic* to escape back to England without answering for their perceived negligence.

Philip Franklin was aware of the senator's pending investigation and convinced Ismay to wait in the USA, along with the crew, until released by Smith. Ismay realised it was best to accept the detention to avoid adverse public opinion and any legal issues an expeditious return might create.

Senator Smith was a member of the Governmental Committee on Commerce and introduced a resolution mandating an investigation into the loss of *Titanic*, which was approved unanimously. His fellow senators appointed him chairman of the new subcommittee to carry out the task.

Although *Titanic* was a British ship, it was owned by IMM, which was an American trust, and it sank with American passengers on board in international waters. Smith assembled a six-man committee, whose members lacked any knowledge of ships or shipping. This was blatantly obvious in some of the questioning.

Though Smith disliked Morgan, he maintained an objectivity that caused many Americans to accept the results, although the press labelled him as a fool and mocked his honest efforts to get the facts. In the end, the press approved of the outcome of the investigation and the subcommittee's recommendations.

The Harter Act of 1898 permitted steamship disaster victims to bring lawsuits against ship owners if it were proved the vessel had been carelessly operated and the owner or operators were aware of the negligence. If Senator Smith could prove there was negligence in the ship's operation, IMM could be sued in the US court for damages due to loss of life and property.

The crew of *Titanic* were berthed aboard *Lapland* and put under guard by agents of the White Star Line. *Lapland* was scheduled to leave for England that coming Saturday, so Smith worked fast. With the approval of President Taft, Smith was able to pick pertinent crew members to subpoena and force them to stay in the USA to testify, including Bruce Ismay, *Titanic*'s four officers and thirty-four crewmen.

Lapland eventually sailed with 167 surviving crew, who were eagerly waiting to go home, arriving at Plymouth on the morning of Sunday, 28 April.

Senator Smith's subcommittee hearings took place over seventeen days between 19 April and 25 May, first convening at New York's Waldorf–Astoria Hotel, then in Washington, D.C. Eighty-two witnesses were heard: fifty-three British subjects or residents, and twenty-nine residents or citizens of the USA. Thirty-four of the ship's crew testified, as did White Star Chairman J. Bruce Ismay, who, despite his efforts to return to England, was compelled to remain for the length of the hearings.

The subcommittee's report, printed on 28 May, three days after the conclusion of the hearings, was about 2,000 pages long. Smith's report praised Captain Rostron and his actions in saving the survivors, and he addressed the shortcomings in the wireless and telegraph communications after the sinking. In the more harshly worded part of the report, Smith condemned Captain Stanley Lord of *Californian* for his failure to respond to distress signals from *Titanic*.

The report's recommendations formed the backbone of the topics discussed at the first International Convention of Safety of Life at Sea (SOLAS), held at London in 1913.

46

White Star Line Paymaster's Uniform Jacket

A White Star Line Paymaster's jacket, which belonged to a member of the Ismay family, is a suitable representation with which to address the pay of *Titanic*'s surviving crew members. The crew signed on to work for a single voyage at an agreed rate of pay which, for transatlantic return trips, was roughly equivalent to a monthly wage paid at the end of the voyage. This rate ranged from £35 ($175) for the chief engineer down to £2 ($10) for the bellboys.

Though some crew members stayed with the same ship for long periods, they were not obliged to sign on for the next voyage, nor was the shipping line obliged to offer them continuous employment. *Titanic*'s crew's pay stopped the moment the ship went down. This was not peculiar to White Star, but general practice for shipping at that time. The White Star Line did, sometime later, make partial payment for the incomplete voyage to surviving crew or to the dependents of those who died.

After the surviving crew members arrived on the *Lapland* at Plymouth, they were ferried ashore on the tender *Sir Richard Grenville*. Upon disembarking, the crew were taken by Board of Trade representatives to a Third Class waiting room, where they were detained until statements could be taken.

The crewmen were ordered not to speak to reporters and were finally released in two groups. First were the seamen and firemen, who boarded a special train for Southampton later that afternoon. The second, consisting of eighty-six stewards, stewardesses and kitchen staff, were released from Plymouth on Tuesday, 30 April. Most boarded another special train for Southampton, where they were greeted by masses of people celebrating their return, while also grieving for those who were lost.

With the intervention of the pertinent unions, White Star agreed to pay the surviving crew for the entire time they had spent away from England. This is seen on the Account of Wages forms as a bonus for the pertinent days' pay. Most of the survivors got a bonus of thirteen days, as they returned to England on 28 April. Those who stayed in the USA for the Senate Inquiry received a quantity more.

47

British Wreck Commissioner's Inquiry and Report on the Loss of SS *Titanic*

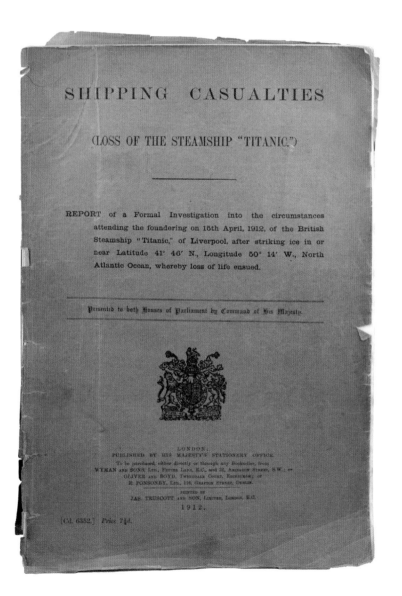

SHIPPING CASUALTIES

(LOSS OF THE STEAMSHIP "TITANIC.")

REPORT of a Formal Investigation into the circumstances attending the foundering on 15th April, 1912, of the British Steamship "Titanic," of Liverpool, after striking ice in or near Latitude 41° 46′ N., Longitude 50° 14′ W., North Atlantic Ocean, whereby loss of life ensued.

Presented to both Houses of Parliament by Command of His Majesty.

LONDON:
PUBLISHED BY HIS MAJESTY'S STATIONERY OFFICE.
To be purchased, either directly or through any Bookseller, from
WYMAN AND SONS, LTD., FETTER LANE, E.C., and 32, ABINGDON STREET, S.W.; or
OLIVER AND BOYD, TWEEDDALE COURT, EDINBURGH; or
E. PONSONBY, LTD., 116, GRAFTON STREET, DUBLIN.

PRINTED BY
JAS. TRUSCOTT AND SON, LIMITED, LONDON, E.C.
1912.

[Cd. 6352.] *Price 7½d.*

While the Americans generally approved of the Senate recommendations, the British did not. In fact, they were quite cross that the US officials took it upon themselves to investigate a British-registered ship. *Titanic* was constructed under the supervision of the British Board of Trade, had operated under the board's regulations and had foundered in international waters.

The British Board of Trade was generally comparable to the US Department of Commerce and was particularly anxious to investigate *Titanic*'s loss on its own. It felt that if any penalties were to be put on the White Star Line, it was the correct jurisdictional authority to do it.

Lord Mersey – Sir John Charles Bigham, Baron Mersey of Toxteth – was appointed Wreck Commissioner, receiving his warrant from Britain's Lord High Chancellor. His five assessors were duly authorised by the Home Secretary. Authority for the inquiry was granted by the Board of Trade itself.

The court sat between 2 May and 3 July. The resulting transcript of the inquiry contained 959 pages, representing 25,622 questions that were asked of ninety-eight witnesses. Nearly the entire inquiry was held at the Drill Hall of the Scottish Regiment, Buckingham Gate, Westminster, London, except for on 6 May, when the court visited the *Olympic* at Southampton, and the last two days of the hearing, when the court convened in London's Caxton Hall.

Published on 30 July, the Board of Trade Inquiry was more extensive than the United States Senate Inquiry. The commission found that the accident was caused by excessive speed, there was an insufficient number of boats and trained men to handle them, and a proper watch was not kept.

The liner's watertight bulkhead design was brought under scrutiny, but then again, the design was approved and constructed to Board of Trade regulations. *Olympic* and *Titanic*'s structural steel specifications reflected their size and exceeded the regulations of the Board of Trade, which were antiquated. (The regulations for ship construction had not been changed since 1894, when the largest vessel afloat was the 12,950-ton

Cunarder *Campania*.) By 1911, the Board of Trade was, for all intents and purposes, investigating its own shortcomings, including the problem with the lack of adequate lifeboat capacity for such vessels with clearance to carry a large number of passengers.

White Star Chairman J. Bruce Ismay was exonerated, and one passenger, Sir Cosmo Duff-Gordon, was found blameless of cowardly behaviour,* the Board of Trade was chided for not updating its 1894 shipping rules, and Captain Rostron received praise for his rescue efforts.

Californian's Captain Stanley Lord was deemed negligent in not coming to *Titanic*'s aid. Captain Lord, for his part, appeared only as a witness. His legal counsel was not given the opportunity to call witnesses who might have verified his statements and attempts to exonerate him were denied in the months and years following the inquiry. It was not until 1992, some thirty years after Lord's death, that a formal investigation based on the location of the wreck site determined that *Californian* was indeed as much as 20 miles from the sinking ship and too far to have made it through the ice field to reach *Titanic* in time.

Concurring with the American report, Mersey's recommendations included twenty-four-hour wireless operation aboard oceangoing ships and frequent lifeboat drills for all crew members. He also called for an international conference to consider the adoption of regulations regarding safety at sea. 'The importance of this Enquiry has to do with the future,' Mersey commented. 'No Enquiry can repair the past.'

The British Inquiry under Lord Mersey found neither J. Bruce Ismay nor Captain Smith guilty of negligence. Claimants who had awaited the inquiry's results, believing their cases had a better chance of succeeding in England, had to now wait for the findings of the Senate Committee in the USA.

---

* Gordon convinced First Officer Murdoch to allow him in Lifeboat No. 1, along with his wife, Lady Duff-Gordon and her secretary, Laura Mabel Francatelli. A few minutes later, Lifeboat No. 1 was lowered containing only twelve people, of whom seven were crew members. Gordon would later offer what was considered by many to be a bribe to the crewman in charge of the lifeboat to not return to the wreck scene in search of survivors.

The United States Southern District Court of New York State had jurisdiction over the petition of the Oceanic Steam Navigation Company Limited (White Star Line) to limit liability as owners of *Titanic*. The court appointed Henry W. Goodrich as commissioner, and he was tasked with reporting the value of *Titanic* regarding all items, except money received from the British Government under mail contracts.

Goodrich's investigation, which included an appraisal of *Titanic*'s lifeboats (the only salvage of worth that remained), prepaid freight and gross monies received from passengers, less expenses such as railway fares and boarding of Third Class passengers, came to a total of £20,159 ($97,772.02). The claims against the Oceanic Steam Navigation Company Limited totalled £3,464,765 ($16,804,112). However, the court had to find whether a claimant's filing was valid, and if so, disperse the funds that were available.

On 22 February 1913, the United States District Court handed down a decision enabling claimants to file suits. With this, the actual liability of the White Star Line had to be determined. This process took the form of liability hearings, which started in June 1915. In 1914, however, a case against the Oceanic Steam Navigation Company in the British courts found negligence in *Titanic*'s navigation – thus causing some claimants to withdraw their cases in the USA and refile them in British courts.

In the end, the amount settled upon to pay out to all claimants was £136,701 ($663,000).

48

Harland & Wolff Correspondence Concerning the Widows of Artie Frost, Robert Knight and Roderick Chisholm

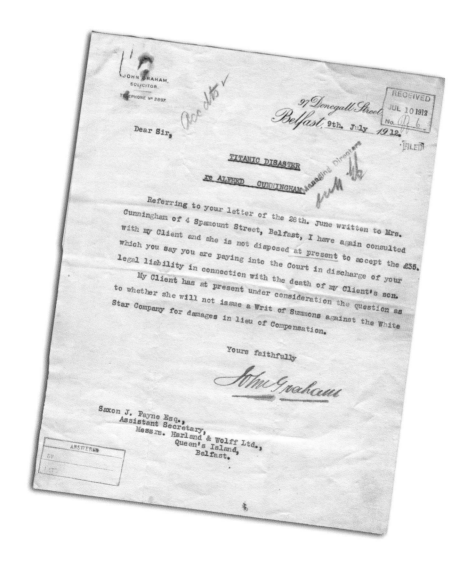

JOHN GRAHAM,
SOLICITOR.
TELEPHONE Nº 2897

Acc dts ✓

97 Donegall Street,
Belfast, 9th. July 1912.

RECEIVED
JUL 10 1912
No.
FILED

Dear Sir,

TITANIC DISASTER

re ALFRED CUNNINGHAM

Managing Directors

Referring to your letter of the 28th. June written to Mrs.
Cunningham of 4 Spamount Street, Belfast, I have again consulted
with my Client and she is not disposed at present to accept the £35.
which you say you are paying into the Court in discharge of your
legal liability in connection with the death of my Client's son.

My Client has at present under consideration the question as
to whether she will not issue a Writ of Summons against the White
Star Company for damages in lieu of Compensation.

Yours faithfully

John Graham

Saxon J. Payne Esq.,
Assistant Secretary,
Messrs. Harland & Wolff Ltd.,
Queen's Island,
Belfast.

ANSWER

BY

1 ST

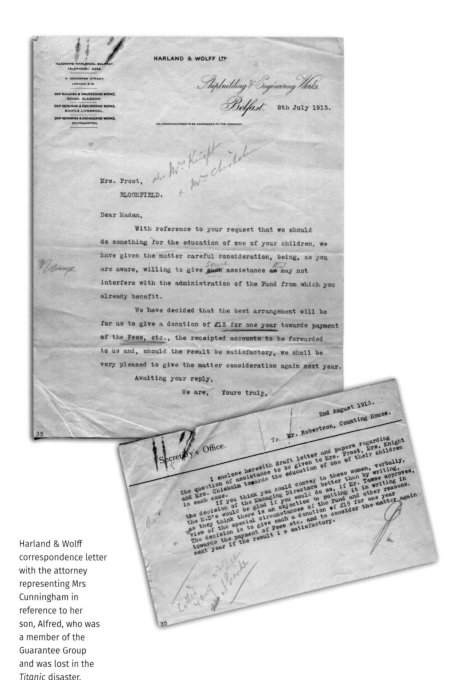

Harland & Wolff correspondence letter with the attorney representing Mrs Cunningham in reference to her son, Alfred, who was a member of the Guarantee Group and was lost in the *Titanic* disaster. (WSM collection)

Elizabeth 'Lizzie' Frost, widow of Anthony Frost of the Harland & Wolff Guarantee Group, had written to the directors asking for assistance in the education of her child. The response was the approval of £15 for one year. If the results obtained were satisfactory, a second year would be paid. The same amount per child was given to the families of Roderick Chisholm and Robert Knight.

The directors of Harland & Wolff sent a letter of sympathy to the Frost family and paid Artie's wages until July 1912. The donation towards education appears to be for all the Frost children, though only one child is mentioned in this letter. Harland & Wolff director, George Cuming, also wrote a letter of sympathy to Artie's father, George, as he too was an employee at Queen's Island before his retirement.

All of the members of the Harland & Wolff Guarantee Group perished on the *Titanic*. The group consisted of men ranging from Managing Director down to apprentices who, it can be assumed, were chosen because of their potential for future advancement. Among the Guarantee Group were some twenty-eight others who were connected with Ulster.

On 26 June 1920, a *Titanic* memorial erected at Donegall Square North was finally dedicated in memory of those Ulstermen lost. The monument was moved in 1959 to Donegall Square East – its present location. Engraved on the pedestal of the monument are the names of the Belfast dead, in order of importance.* The first eight names are those of the Harland & Wolff Guarantee Group:

Thomas Andrews – Managing Director; William H.M. Parr – Assistant Manager Electrical Department; Roderick Chisholm – Chief Draughtsman; Anthony Wood Frost – Foreman Fitter; Robert Knight – Leading Hand Fitter; William Campbell – Apprentice Joiner; Ennis H. Watson – Apprentice Electrician; Francis Parkes – Apprentice Plumber; Alfred F. Cunningham – Apprentice Fitter.**

---

* It was the practice in the era prior to the First World War to list names in order of rank/importance.
** Cameron, Stephen, *Titanic: Belfast's Own* (Dublin: Wolfhound Press, 1998).

49

First Paperback Edition of *A Night to Remember* (1956)

This first paperback edition of Walter Lord's *A Night to Remember* was printed by Bantam Books in 1956. The binding is broken and the pages dog-eared. It was in the possession of a *Titanic* historian for years and, as can be seen, it has been well used.

In 1912, *Titanic* was in everyone's thoughts, and everyone, it seemed, had an opinion or suggestion for keeping ocean travel safe. The newspapers and trade publications were filled with commentaries from novice to professional, whether it be who was to blame for *Titanic*'s sinking or how to keep this type of incident from happening again. Relief organisations and charities were set up – too many to mention here – for the assistance of people affected by the *Titanic*'s demise. Memorials were dedicated to the deceased. Statues and plaques were unveiled, saluting individuals such as Major Archibald Butt, journalist W.T. Stead, Mr and Mrs Isidor Straus, and Captain Edward J. Smith.

However, interest began to wane as the decades wore on, except for the occasional observance or magazine article. Certainly, two world wars distracted people, with other situations taking precedence.

Titanic was, however, kept alive by devoted hobbyists, archivists and historians. In 1955, journalist Walter Lord published his book *A Night to Remember*, depicting the sinking of *Titanic* on 15 April 1912. The book was hugely successful, and is still considered a definitive resource about the *Titanic*. It is prerequisite reading for anyone who considers themselves a *Titanic* historian.

Lord interviewed sixty-three survivors of the disaster as well as drawing on books, memoirs and articles that they had written. In 1986, Lord authored his follow-up book, *The Night Lives On*, following renewed interest in the story after the wreck of the *Titanic* had been discovered by Robert Ballard the year before.

Lord travelled on *Olympic* when he was a boy, and the experience gave him a lifelong fascination with the lost *Titanic*. He later reminisced how he spent his time on *Olympic* 'prowling around' and trying to imagine 'such a huge thing' sinking. He started reading about and drawing *Titanic* at the age of 10, spending many years collecting *Titanic* memorabilia.

A Night to Remember was adapted twice for the silver screen. The first production was in 1956, staged as a live adaptation on 28 March 1956 by NBC TV. The second adaptation was the 1958 British drama film *A Night to Remember*, starring Kenneth More and produced by William MacQuitty, which is widely regarded as the definitive cinematic telling of the story.

After Lord died in 2002, he bequeathed to the National Maritime Museum in Greenwich, England, his huge collection of manuscripts, original letters and *Titanic* memorabilia, which he had gathered during his life and used as reference to write *A Night to Remember*. *Titanic* enthusiast groups and societies grew out of the work undertaken originally by Walter Lord, and now exist in many countries on both sides of the Atlantic Ocean, the earliest being the 1963-formed *Titanic* Historical Society in Indian Orchard, Massachusetts.

In 1991, members of Titanic International, a *Titanic* history group based in Freehold, New Jersey, used recovery records and information from other sources to identify six of the forty-two previously unknown victims who were buried in Halifax. With appropriate ceremony, their headstones, originally supplied by the White Star Line in 1912, were unveiled in September of that year, finally bearing their names after almost eight decades of being classified as 'unknown'. Today, the city of Halifax has assumed responsibility for the upkeep of the graves. A White Star Line trust fund was established in 1912 and was apparently once supplemented by Cunard, which merged with White Star in 1934. It maintains the stones in perpetuity, aided by donations from around the world.

Titanic has been featured in numerous films, TV movies and notable TV episodes. As for theatrical released cinematic dramas about *Titanic*, there are some eighteen instances, either about *Titanic* specifically or including her within a larger storyline, from 1912 through to 2018. Documentaries produced about *Titanic* are too many to mention.

50

White Star Line Officer's Hat Used in the 1997 Epic Film *Titanic*

James Cameron brought *Titanic* into full colour for the world. His film technology and use of actual wreck dive footage intertwined with matching film sets, staging for a fictional romance, and weaving in and out of historically factual situations, sparked the emotions of almost everyone who saw the film.

The film *Titanic* was written, produced and co-edited by Cameron himself. It won eleven Academy Awards and initially grossed $1.84 billion – the first film to reach the $1 billion mark.

Shown here is a White Star Line officer's hat prop that was part of the many costumes used in the film; the sets and props were heavily researched and produced with the consultation of world-renowned *Titanic* historians.

Cameron's *Titanic* jump-started the next wave of *Titanic* historians and enthusiasts, and was influential around the world and even in China. Though the movie is a fictional romance, the back story was so heavily researched and well done that it is, for many, more influential than MacQuitty's 1958 *A Night to Remember*.

In the years that followed the release of *Titanic*, James Cameron returned to the wreck site multiple times, filming more footage inside the wreck than ever before. His work is responsible for revealing many mysteries about the operational aspects of *Titanic*.

Acknowledgements

To Charlie Haas and the late Jack Eaton for *Triumph and Tragedy*. '*T&T*' has always been one of my main references. Pulling it off the shelf for *Titanic in 50 Objects* ('*Tin50*') reminded me, just as it did twenty-five years ago, that you two seemed to have put everything you had into that work. It is as complete as it can be in representing the *Titanic* timeline.

Thank you to David Scott-Beddard and John White, owners of White Star Memories Ltd, for their friendship and for allowing the use of their artefacts in this book, and also to Bob Angel of the British Titanic Society for his contributions of artefacts.

Thank you to Clive Sweetingham of the British Titanic Society, the photographer of most of the White Star Memories artefacts.

I am grateful to Cathy Akers-Jordan for editing *Titanic in 50 Objects* and writing the foreword, and to Brian Thompson – friend and personal photographer – who has travelled with me to the UK and China on assignment.

Thank you to William Young, who was quick in supplying me reference material from his collection and is one of my most trusted ocean liner history experts.

My grateful thanks to my chief, Steve Orlando and my general manager, Michael Phillips of the Residence Inn, Lakeland.

I'd like to offer a special word of thanks to my wife, Michele Beveridge, who has assisted in writing this book, providing support, suggestions and allowing me time away from our normal life activities, and to my children, William, Sarah, Scott, Stephen, Spencer, Noelle, Sarah II and Michael.

To my late-night office assistant, Apollo, thank you.

My mother, Jane Crawford, undertook a *Titanic* journey with me in 2017 and has always supported my endeavours.

Ray Lepien – the historian extraordinaire and the walrus with the longest tusks.

Craig Mestach – for his everlasting support.

Steve and Bruce together would like to thank:

Scott Andrews, Daniel Klistorner and Art Braunschweiger for being old writing partners, and for always being there when needed.

The staff of The History Press, and in particular, Amy Rigg, Martin Latham, Katie Beard and Jezz Palmer, who have worked closely with us on our many *Titanic* projects, and who have somehow always managed to remain calm during the many requests for deadline extensions.

And finally, to all of our fellow *Titanic* researchers, including close friends, who have inspired us, whether they know it or not.

References

Bäbler, Günter, *Guide to the Crew of Titanic* (The History Press, 2017).

Beesley, Lawrence, *The Loss of the SS Titanic* (Haughton Mifflin Co., 1912).

Beveridge, Bruce, et al., *Titanic: the Ship Magnificent, Vol. I* (The History Press, 2008).

—*Titanic: the Ship Magnificent, Vol. II* (The History Press, 2008).

Chirnside, Mark, *RMS Olympic* (The History Press, 2015).

—*The Olympic-Class Ships* (Tempus Publishing Ltd, 2004).

Eaton, John P., and Charles A. Haas, *Titanic: Destination Disaster* (W.W. Norton & Company, 1996).

—*Titanic, Triumph and Tragedy* (W.W. Norton & Company, 1995).

Hall, Steve, Beveridge, Bruce, and Art Braunschweiger, *Titanic or Olympic: Which Ship Sank?* (The History Press, 2012).

Halpern, Samuel, et al., *Report into the Loss of the Titanic* (The History Press, 2016).

'Harland and Wolff's Works at Belfast', *Engineering*, Vol. 94, 5 July 1912: 3–50.

Klistorner, Daniel, et al., *Titanic in Photographs* (The History Press, 2011).

O'Donnell, Eugene, Edward, and Frank Browne, *The Last Days of the Titanic* (Roberts Rinehart Publishing, 1997).

'The White Star Liners "Olympic" and "Titanic"', *Engineering*, Vol. 91, 26 May 1911.

US Senate Documents (No. 726, 62nd Congress, 2nd Session), 'Hearings into the loss of the SS Titanic, 19 April–25 May 1912'.

US Senate Report (No. 806, 62nd Congress, 2nd Session) of the Committee on Commerce, 'The Titanic Disaster' [AI Report], 28 May 1912.

Wels, Susan, *Titanic: Legacy of the World's Greatest Ocean Liner* (Time Life Education, 1997).

Wreck Commissioner's Court, 'Proceedings on the Formal Investigation Ordered by the Board of Trade into the Loss of the SS Titanic, 2 May–3 July 1912'.

Web References

Thomas Andrews – 'Encyclopedia Titanica' (2017), ref: #8, last updated 18 August 2017: www.encyclopedia-titanica.org/titanic-victim/thomas-andrews.html

Molly Brown and Captain Rostron – 'Encyclopedia Titanica' (2003), ref: #1054, published 28 August 2003: www.encyclopedia-titanica.org/molly-brown-presenting-loving-cup-captain-arthur-rostron.html

Anthony Wood Frost – 'Encyclopedia Titanica' (2018), ref: #415, last updated 4 July 2018: www.encyclopedia-titanica.org/titanic-victim/anthony-wood-frost.html

Robert Knight – 'Encyclopedia Titanica' (2019), ref: #480, last updated 9 May 2019: www.encyclopedia-titanica.org/titanic-victim/robert-knight.html

Index

A Night to Remember 228–30
Adriatic 21, 30
Ah Lam 189
Algerine 211
Allison, Hudson J.C. 107
America 51, 115–16, 121, 212
American Line 21
Amerika 161
Anderson, Fr Roger 203
Andrews, Thomas 26, 31, 99,
    171–2, 227
Antillian 163–4
Aspinall, Butler 185–7, 192
Astor, Col. John Jacob 110, 189
Astor, Madeline Force 110, 202
Athenai 161
Atlantic Transport Line 21

Bailey, Henry, Master-at-Arms 185
Baker, Bernard N. 21
Ballard, Dr Robert, 156, 229
Baltic 21, 80, 161
Barker, Reginald, Second Purser 160
Baron de Hirsch Cemetery 211
Barrett, Frederick, Head Stoker
    171, 187
Becker, Ruth 188
Beesley, Lawrence 105, 116, 181,
    183, 187
Bell, Joseph, Chief Engineer 77, 96,
    159, 194
Bigham, Sir John Charles 222
binoculars 87–9
Bishop, Dickinson 111, 183–4, 206
Bishop, Helen 111, 184, 206
Blair, David, Second Officer 77, 88
Bowyer, George, Trinity House
    Harbour Pilot 101
Bowyer, Henry, Mayor of
    Southampton 213
Boxhall, Joseph Grove, Fourth
    Officer 77, 88, 94, 117, 158, 161,
    171, 176–7, 180, 188, 199
Brailey, Theodore 105

Brandeis, Emil 110
Bricoux, Roger 105
Bride, Harold, Marconi Operator
    77–8, 97, 116, 164, 175–6,
    189, 204
Bright, Arthur, Quartermaster 190
Britannic 19, 29–30, 68, 178
British Board of Trade 41, 54, 78, 101,
    220, 222–3
Brown, Ernest G.F., Chief Purser 22,
    25, 204, 215
Brown, Margaret 111, 214–16
Browne, Francis 56, 115–17, 172, 175–6
Buley, Edward, Able-Bodied
    Seaman 188
Butt, Major Archibald, 107, 163,
    183, 229
Byles, Fr Thomas 160

Californian 163, 166, 177, 203–4,
    218, 223
Cameron, James 231–2
Campania 54–5, 223
Campbell, William 99, 227
Carlisle, Alexander M. 26, 31–2, 37, 212
Caronia 159
Carpathia 94–5, 176, 194–6, 198–9,
    201–4, 206, 208–10, 214–16
Carruthers, Francis 78
Carter, William 189
Cedric 21, 206
Celtic (I) 19
Celtic (II) 21, 80
Chang Chip 189
Chart Room 89, 161
Cherbourg 30, 37, 82, 108–12, 114–15,
    178, 180
Chisholm, Roderick 99, 225, 227
Clarke, Capt. Maurice 101, 105
Coffey, John, Stoker 115
Collyer, Charlotte 187
Coronia 160
Cottam, Harold, Marconi Operator
    195–6, 198, 204

CQD 94, 175–6, 196, 205
Crighton, Robert 26
Crosby, Sir Thomas Boor, Lord
    Mayor of London 213
Cuming, George 26, 227
Cunard Line 22–3, 25, 30, 51, 54,
    178, 195, 206, 215, 230
Cunningham, Alfred F. 99, 227

Dean, Horace, First Officer 196
Dominion Line 22
Duff-Gordon, Sir Cosmo 110
Duff-Gordon, Lady 111, 223
Duke of Argyll 46
Dymond, Frank, Fireman 188

Ellerman, John 22
Evans, Cyril, Marconi Operator
    158–9, 166

Fairview Cemetery 211
Fang Lang 194–5
Fastnet Light 121
Fenwick, Mabel 201
Fleet, Frederick, Lookout 158,
    162, 166–7
Fletcher, Peter W. 127
Frankfurt 175
Franklin, Philip 202, 206, 216
Frost, Anthony 'Artie' Wood 98–9,
    225, 227
Frost, Elizabeth 'Lizzie' 98, 227
Frost, George W. 99
Futrelle, Jacques 107, 116

Gatti, Luigi 101, 137
Gee, Arthur 109
Germanic 19
Gibson, Dorothy 111
Giglio, Victor 184
Glenravel 36, 38
Goldsmith, Emily 189
Goldsmith, Frank 65, 175, 183,
    188–9, 202
Goodrich, W. 224
Gracie, Col. Archibald 107, 143, 160
Griscom, Clement 21
Guggenheim, Benjamin 110, 184

Haddock, Capt. Herbert James 77
Haines, Albert, Boatswain's Mate 187
Halifax 203, 205, 210–11, 230

Hamburg–America Line 22
Hankinson, Thomas, Chief
    Officer 198
Hardy, John, Chief Second Class
    Steward 204
Harland & Wolff 17–18, 24–6, 30–2,
    34–41, 44–8, 57, 59, 61, 63, 66,
    82, 98–9, 110–11, 157, 171, 180,
    212, 225–7
    Guarantee Group 98–9, 157,
        171, 226–7
Harland, Edward J. 25
Harmer, Abraham (David
    Livshin) 203
Harper, Henry 184
Harris, Henry B. 107
Harrison, William Henry 102, 158
Hart, John, Steward 181
Hartley, Wallace 105, 193–4
Hemming, Samuel, Lamp
    Trimmer 162
Herculaneum 77
Hercules 77, 82
Hesketh, John, Second Engineer 171
Hichens, Robert, Quartermaster
    165–6, 170, 185
Hippach, Ida 107
Hippach, Jean 107
Hogg, George, Lookout 88,
    158–9, 184
Hornby 77
Hoskins & Sewell Ltd 69
Hoyt, William F. 203
Hume, John Law 105
Humphreys, Sidney, Able-Bodied
    Seaman 187
Huskisson 77

Imperator 30
Imrie, William 18
International Convention of Safety
    of Life at Sea (SOLAS), 218
International Mercantile Marine
    Co. (IMM) 21–22, 158, 202,
    208, 216–17
Isle of Wight 82, 112
Ismay, Imrie & Co. 18–19
Ismay, J. Bruce 19–22, 29, 37, 46,
    100, 102, 161, 189, 200, 202,
    206, 208, 217, 223
Ismay, Thomas Henry 17–21, 59

J.P. Morgan & Co. 21
Jewell, Archibald, Lookout 158–9,
        162, 166
John Brown & Co. Ltd 22, 25
Jones, Thomas, Able-Bodied
        Seaman 185

Kempster, W. 26
Keyzar, Rupert 180
Knight, Robert 99, 225, 227
Krins, Georges Alexander 105

La Provence 175
Lapland 208–9, 217, 220
Lard, Capt. Stanley 166, 223
Laroche, Joseph 111
Lee Bing 189
Lee, Reginald, Lookout 158, 162,
        166–7, 189
Leyland Line 22, 177
Lightoller, Charles Herbert,
        Second Officer 77, 88, 92–3,
        158, 162, 164, 166, 170, 173,
        180, 184–5, 188–9, 192, 202,
        204
Ling Hee 189
Liverpool 17, 19, 46, 53, 61, 77,
        80, 82, 94–5, 105, 159, 161,
        213, 215
Loeb, William 208
Lord, Capt. Stanley 218, 223
Lord, Walter 229-230
Lowe, Harold Godfrey, Fourth
        Officer 77, 88, 94–6, 101, 117,
        158–9, 161, 173, 180, 184–8,
        194, 200, 202–3
Lusitania 22–3, 25, 29–30, 51
Lyons, William, Able-Bodied
        Seaman 203

McCawley, T.W. 116
McElroy, Hugh, Chief Purser 186
McGee, Dr Frank 202
McGough, George, Able-Bodied
        Seaman 187
McGrady, James, Steward 211
MacQuitty, William 230, 232
Mackay-Bennett 193, 210
Magnetic 20
Majestic 19, 30, 93
Mallet family 111
Mansion House 212–13

Marconi Company 41, 55–6, 77–8,
        97, 116, 157–8, 166, 174–6,
        189–90, 204
Marshall, Ken 57
Mauretania 22, 25, 29–30, 51
Merchant Shipping Acts 101
Mersey 18, 20, 222–3
Mesaba 164
Millet, Frank 183
Mills, Christopher, Assistant
        Butcher 85
Minia 210
Montmagny 210
Montvila, Fr Juozas 160
Moody, James Paul, Sixth Officer
        88, 95–6, 101, 117, 158, 161, 166,
        168, 173, 180, 185, 187–8, 190
More, Kenneth 230
Morgan, J. Pierpont 21, 46, 216–17
Mount Temple 175
Mt Olivet Cemetery 211
Mulvihill, Bertha 188
Murdoch, William M., First Officer
        77, 87, 91–3, 95, 162, 166, 168,
        170–1, 173, 180, 184, 187–90, 223

Nab Lightship 82
Nantucket Shoals Lightvessel 121
National Line 18
Nomadic 37, 46, 110–12, 178, 180
        Nomadic Preservation Society 180
        Savenomadic.com 178, 180
Noordam 160
North German Lloyd line 22
Northern Ireland Department of
        Social Development 180

O'Loughlin, William, Ships'
        Surgeon 101
Oceanic 17-20, 30, 77, 93–5, 107,
        211, 224
Oceanic Steam Navigation
        Company 17, 224
Olliver, Alfred, Quartermaster 165–7
Olympic passim

Painton, James A. 127
Parisian 195
Parkes, Francis 99, 227
Parr, William 99, 227
Perkis, Walter, Quartermaster 188
Peruschitz, Fr Josef 160

Phillips, John 'Jack', Marconi
    Operator 77–8, 97, 164, 166,
    175–6, 189–90
Pickard, Berk 181
Pirrie, Lord William J. 25–6, 29, 31,
    37, 46, 212
Pitman, Herbert John, Third Officer
    77, 88, 90, 93, 117, 158–9, 161,
    180, 184
Poingdestre, John, Able-Bodied
    Seaman 187
Pratten, W.J. 26
Pritchard, Mervyn 180

Queen Elizabeth 178
Queen Mary 30, 178, 180

Red Star Line 21
Rencher, Gottlieb 202
Robert Hickson & Co. 25
Robinson, Maria 193
Roche's Point 115
Rostron, Capt. Arthur 195–6, 198–9,
    201–4, 214–16, 218, 223
Rothes, Countess 107
Rowe, George, Quartermaster
    94, 189
Russell, Edith 111
Ryerson family 110

Sanderson, Harold Arthur 19, 100
Schwabe, Gustavas C. 17
Scott-Beddard, David 178, 180
Seward, Frederick K. 215
Siebert, Sidney C., Bedroom
    Steward 203
Simpson, Edward J., Assistant
    Surgeon 101
Sir Richard Grenville 220
Smith, Capt. Edward John 77, 79–81,
    87, 92, 94, 101, 108, 127, 156,
    159–64, 166, 171, 175–6, 180,
    184, 186, 188, 190–2, 223, 229
Smith, Senator William
    Alden 216–17
Solomon, Henry 33
SOS 176
Southampton *passim*
Spedden family 117

Spencer, Heath & George Ltd 143
Spicer-Simson, Theodore 214–15
Stanton, Samuel Ward 111
Stead, W.T. 229
Steele, Capt. Benjamin 101
Stewart, C.J. 213
Straus, Ida 107, 185
Straus, Isidor 185, 229
Swan, Hunter & Wigham
    Richardson Ltd 22, 24
Symons, George, Lookout 158–9,
    162, 166, 185

Taft, President William H. 107, 217
Taylor, Percy, Second Purser 105, 204
Teutonic 19, 30, 77
Thayer, John 'Jack' Borland 111, 192
Thayer, Marion 111
The Night Lives On 229
Titanic passim
    Belfast visitor attraction 180
    Titanic Historical Society 230
    Titanic International 230
Traffic 37, 110, 112
Train Transatlantique 110

Von Drachstedt, Baron Alfred
    (Alfred Nourney) 111
Vulcan 82, 108

Watson, Ennis 99
Watson, Ennis H. 227
Wennerstrom, August 190
White Star Line *passim*
White Swan Hotel 133
White, John 178
Widener, George D. 163
Wilde, Henry Tingle, Chief Officer
    87, 91, 93, 158, 162, 172, 180,
    184–5, 188–9
Wilding, Edward 26
Wilkinson, Norman 131
Wilson & Company 19
Wilson, Alexander B. 26
Wilson, Walter H. 26
Wolff, Gustav W. 17, 25–6
Woodward, John Wesley 105
Wright, Fred 114, 143